Praise for Not Over Yet

Stephanie is beautifully transparent with her journey, offering practical solutions, encouragement, hope, and God's truth to single mothers everywhere. A must-read!

~ Ammie Bouwman, author of *In Over My Head*, *Finding Joy Again*, *The Hidden Door*, and more

Not Over Yet is a beautiful, easy read. One that made me feel positive and powerful! It was like putting on God's love and grace.

~ Sara Clark, single mom

Not Over Yet

a single mom's guide to reclaiming hope

Stephanie Bartelt

5 am light Press

Waukesha, Wisconsin

Unless otherwise noted, Scripture quotations taken from The Holy Bible, New International Version® NIV®
Copyright © 1973 1978 1984 2011 by Biblica, Inc. ™
Used by permission. All rights reserved worldwide.

Where noted, Scripture taken from the New King James Version. Copyright © 1982 by Thomas Nelson, Inc. Used by permission. All rights reserved.

Where noted, Scripture quotations are from The ESV® Bible (The Holy Bible, English Standard Version®), copyright © 2001 by Crossway, a publishing ministry of Good News Publishers. Used by permission. All rights reserved.

Interior Design: Stephanie Bartelt
Cover Design: Stephanie Bartelt

ISBN: 979-8-9867708-0-2

5 am light Press
Waukesha, WI

Printed in the United States of America

Library of Congress Control Number: 2022916403

Not Over Yet is dedicated to my mom
who was my backup driver, meal dropper-offer,
and biggest cheerleader. She loved all of
her grandchildren relentlessly.

We miss you, Mom.

Let the redeemed of the Lord say so,
whom he has redeemed from trouble.

Psalm 107:2 (ESV)

Contents

Prologue

The day my husband came back to get his things was worse than any day I could imagine. I had spent weeks carefully dividing up our belongings and packing all his into boxes; now, I helped him carry the boxes down three flights of stairs to load in his car. My feet felt heavy and awkward, as if I was trying to walk through shifting sand.

After he left, I willed myself to hold it together until our then three-year-old daughter took her nap. I quietly closed the door to her room and the floodgates opened. I slid down the smooth plaster wall and sat sobbing on the floor in the hallway, willing myself to grieve soundlessly.

I was devastated. Panic flooded over me. My mind raced with questions as I shook with grief. Could I support us? Where would we live? How could I raise a child all on my own? Would she ever see her dad again? Why didn't he want us?

I was raised in a Christian home and had fully planned on being married forever. And here I was, suddenly a single mom, living hours away from my family, disconnected from friends. I had never felt so alone.

That day, as I had helped him load the car, he had said, with great disdain, "Sorry I ruined your life." In that moment, something stirred deep inside me. Something that had survived the years of neglect. And I heard myself say, quietly and firmly, "My life isn't over yet."

My life isn't over yet.

And neither is yours.

No matter what dire situation you are in, there is One who is waiting to carry you through. To hold your head up as the waters rise. To be the barrier between you and the flames. To hold you and heal your deep wounds.

Jesus carried me through and used my desperate circumstances to mold me and shape me and prune me into who He created me to be. He's still working on me. My prayer is that the truths He revealed to me will help you find that place deep inside where you know that your life isn't over yet, either.

In truth, maybe life is just beginning.

CHAPTER 1

Not Forgotten

I see you. Even now. Hiding under the covers, curled up on the sofa, hiding in the closet with chocolate.

I see your deep hurts and fears. I see the pain of trying to get up each day and keep moving for your kids. I see you holding back tears until little hearts are tucked safely in bed.

I hear your fears for the future bouncing around in my own head, as I heard my own fears years ago. And I am here to tell you that you can do this. You can do this thing that seems impossible. With God's help, you can pick up the pieces of your life and move forward. You can build a bright, amazing future for yourself and your children.

You may feel powerless, uncertain, and forgotten right now. Emotions can get the best of us, and our fears and thoughts can run wild. It's critical to remember the truths found in God's Word. God's power is in you. God knows your past, present, and future. God has not forgotten you. He could never forget you. It's not in His character to forget His children. "Can a mother forget the baby at her breast and have no compassion on the child she has borne? Though she may forget, I will not forget you!" (Isaiah 49:15).

He knows exactly where you are, what you're going through, and where He's going to take you. He promises He won't ever leave you. "The LORD himself goes before you and will be with you; he will never leave you nor forsake you. Do not be afraid; do not be discouraged" (Deuteronomy 31:8).

Right now, that may be hard to imagine. If you've been hurt or left by someone who promised to love you forever, you may feel completely forgotten and abandoned. It might be hard to imagine being safe and secure in God's love. But His love is infinitely better than any human love. He is filled with compassion for you. His love for you reaches to the heavens. He is the ultimate promise keeper. He can't do anything other than what He says He will do.

You are the apple of His eye. His treasure. His beloved.

He proved it in my life. God knew the struggles that were coming my way and the isolation I would experience. He knew what every day would bring, and He allowed it, but He didn't leave me alone in it. He prepared people ahead of time, connected me to others again, and had a plan in place that I couldn't have written if I tried.

Looking back, I can see His fingerprints everywhere. But in those moments, I was blinded by the thick fog surrounding me. You may be in that same place—not knowing what the future holds or how you can forge a path ahead. And let me share with you that your future is worth the effort. Worth putting bare, worn feet, one in front of the other. God promises to be the light for our path, but He never says He will light it up all at once.

Sometimes it's our job to keep walking as He lights up one more step.

Once I turned to Him, this God who loves us enough to send His son on the ultimate rescue mission—the only rescue mission that is able to fully redeem a life—began filling my mind with His truth: the great God of the universe had not forgotten me.

He hasn't forgotten you, either. He chose you. He wants you. He thought of you before the beginning of the world and decided to make you for His pleasure. To be His companion. You are the apple of His eye. His treasure. His beloved. No one on this earth can ever love you as much as He does.

Maybe you have been hiding from Him, ashamed of your choices or of what has been done to you.

Maybe you have been running from Him, not knowing how to turn back. None of that, nothing in the world, has changed His love for you. He is waiting with open arms.

As you walk through this valley, this struggle, remember that you are never walking alone. He is everything we could ever need, and He will provide for us. He met me in my darkest moments and never let go. I promise He'll hold on to you if you let Him.

Let's follow Him together.

Connections
Are you feeling abandoned or forgotten by God or others?

First Step Forward
Search out three Bible verses that remind you that God has not forgotten you. Write them out and put them up around your house to help you remember His love for you.

1.

2.

3.

CHAPTER 2

The Slow Fade

Let me tell you a bit of my story.

Our little family is just me, my two daughters, our dog, and an ever-changing number of fish. My older daughter was born eleven years into my marriage, and I adopted my younger daughter from Uganda several years after my marriage ended.

I grew up in a Christian home with loving parents and attended Faith Community Church, a wonderful, Bible-believing church, in a beautiful brick building with intricate old lights and windows. We went to church three times a week: Sunday morning, Sunday night, and Wednesday night. For several years I won all of the Sword Drills in Sunday School (a contest to see who could find a Bible verse first). I remember looking up to the older generation (literally and figuratively) while racing around the church after Sunday morning service, entertaining myself while the parents talked for what seemed like hours. I didn't really mind because I felt so safe and happy in that place. Anywhere I wanted to play was okay. And everywhere I went, there was an adult who would lovingly put me in my place if needed.

I loved Pastor Powell's voice and Mr. Sorrell's joy when he played the piano. Mr. Sorrell couldn't read music but played the piano like a virtuoso. I won a costume contest during AWANA one year when my mom and I made a costume of Oscar the Grouch. (By the way, it is impossible to sit while wearing a garbage can made out of cardboard covered in tinfoil.) My childhood was great.

I planned to grow up, get married, have children, and be a missionary with my forever husband. When I was eight years old, I went forward during an altar call for anyone who felt called to serve Jesus around the world. I went to youth group and prayer and praise nights and loved Jesus with my whole heart.

Then we moved and had to leave our amazing church. Middle school and high school came, and the slow fade began. I loved God with everything in me, but I had bad experiences with people in church. I grew old enough and mature enough to see that not all Christians were who I thought they were. I was not yet wise enough to look past them and keep my eyes on my Savior.

When I went to college, there weren't any churches that I could get to easily. The one I loved was an hour away by foot. It was a treat to attend, but I certainly wasn't committed enough to walk an hour in the freezing cold and snow of winter. So, without noticing, without intention, I took another step away from God. Eventually, I wandered far enough from Him that I couldn't see the truth anymore.

The Long Way Home

I married my husband the fall after graduation. We eventually moved to a big city, far enough from family and friends that we couldn't visit often, and in a time of our lives that made it hard to meet new people. Suddenly, fifteen years had passed since I had regularly attended church.

I had tried several churches in our area over the years, but I felt unsettled in every single one. I felt like I was watching a show, and they had put a spotlight on me in the audience—trapped, uncomfortable, keenly aware that I didn't belong. I wondered if I had been gone from church for too long and wouldn't ever feel a part of one again. But God was drawing me back to Him. No matter how awkward and uncomfortable I had felt the week before, come Sunday, I again wished I was in church.

Light started breaking into my darkness when my little girl was finally born after many years of waiting. When she was 18 months old, I mustered up the courage to walk into a church I had driven by and wondered about for many years. It was a beautiful small brick building with steep angles on the roof and lovely stained-glass windows above the doors. I felt drawn to this building and wondered if I would fit in on the other side of those doors.

I trudged up the five brick steps and in through the glass front doors. I stood frozen, barely inside, fighting the urge to run back out. I didn't know how to find my way back to a church family after so long. I held my breath and ran my eyes over everything, trying to get my bearings.

A woman approached me smiling, asked how she could help and led me in the direction of the nursery. Since none of the nursery workers had arrived yet, she signed in my daughter and told me she would stay with her until the others arrived so I wouldn't miss the service.

I thanked her and proceeded to the sanctuary, an open space with a soaring ceiling and beautiful stained-glass windows lining one wall.

After I sat down, I was in utter disbelief that I had just handed my daughter over to a complete stranger and walked away. That child was my everything. The only good thing I could see in my life.

Several times during the service, I almost got up to check on her, but something kept me still, fixed to that wooden pew that was worn smooth by countless others before me. I have no idea what the sermon was that day. No idea what songs were sung. But I sure remember the feeling of coming home, of being safe from the storm for an hour.

The next Sunday, and the Sunday after that, I returned to that little church. I was embarrassed to be the married woman sitting alone in church, wishing my husband was there with me. I kept my home life hidden, but church gave me much-needed rest and replenishment every week. It was refreshing for my soul in so many ways. I had missed being able to praise God with others and sit under steady biblical teaching. I had missed taking communion to honor Christ's sacrifice for me. I was finally able to meet other people who believed as I did and wanted to live life in community. I had been lonely for so many years and now saw potential friends all around me.

I found people who loved my daughter and me well. I found moments of hope I hadn't felt in ages.

God met me in those long days and months. For years, He had been waiting for me to want Him again. For me to see that He was the only answer to the struggles I was going through. And as I kept returning to church week after week, He started tenderly treating my wounds. He began to pick up the pieces of my life and hold them in His hands.

Reminding me that no matter what I see, He sees it all.

Reminding me He has a plan beyond my comprehension.

Reminding me how very loved I am, even though I hadn't felt loved in years. Reminding me that His love is what matters, that He created me with a beautiful purpose in mind, and all of the lies the world could feed me are nothing in light of the truth of who God says I am.

If you have a personal relationship with Jesus, if he is your Savior, the same is true for you.

Remember what He calls you. Chosen. Adopted. Redeemed. Worthy. Adored.

When He sees you returning, even taking one step in His direction, He will come running to meet you. Running! His love for you is immeasurable, unending, and filled with grace. It is never too late.

You are chosen. You are adopted. You are redeemed. You are worthy. You are adored.

Come home.

> All of the lies the world can feed us are nothing in light of the truth of who God says we are.

Connections

What is stopping you from finding your church home,
and how can you overcome it?

First Step Forward

If you don't have a church home, list three churches you
could try and choose which one to go to this week.

1.

2.

3.

CHAPTER 3

The Struggle

I joined a Bible study at my new church with four other ladies. We met every Saturday morning and shared our struggles. Except for me. I still kept my real life concealed.

The girl who had given her life to Christ at age six and had planned to be a missionary couldn't possibly be the same girl who was living this life. The girl who had always wanted to be a mom had suffered from infertility and a miscarriage and was now a mom in a crumbling marriage. I was ashamed and hiding the brokenness of my marriage from everyone, having no idea what the future would hold. I had planned on being married forever. Divorce had never crossed my mind, even on the hardest days. I had promised for better or worse and meant it. Now I didn't know how long I could survive like this.

One day I saw a message on a computer screen I was never intended to see. My whole body began to tremble. My brain went blank. My only thought was to get to church. Like a lighthouse in the storm, the building drew me in. I didn't call before I went, just prayed that I could drive safely even with the tremors in my body. And that the pastor would be there.

I unbuckled my then three-year-old and carried her into church. The sweet ladies in the office took care of my precious girl while I walked down the long hall to the pastor's office.

Dropping my bag on the floor and my body into the padded wooden chair, I could hardly breathe. The room melted away, and all I could see were my hands clenched in my lap and my pastor listening intently on the other side of the desk. Details of my life over the last few years dropped one by one from my lips. I felt myself shaking, taking deep breaths to find the strength to continue.

I told him enough of the story. All I could admit to at that moment. More of my story than anyone else knew.

As my story unfolded, Pastor Brown leaned back in his chair, soaking in my words and murmuring in understanding. This story was familiar to him, and I could see pain in his eyes from hearing it again. His compassion, his willingness to enter my grief with me, helped me realize that my situation was every bit as bad as it felt. I wasn't exaggerating or being dramatic. This wasn't how marriage was supposed to be.

When I finished, Pastor Brown leaned in and spoke words that were a balm to my soul. He said that if my husband left, I could rest in knowing that I did my best to save my marriage. I leaned hard on those words over the years, wanting, needing them to be true. I still battled feelings of guilt— wondering what I could have done differently. During times of questioning and wishing my marriage had survived, I pulled those words out from deep in my heart, and I continue to speak that truth over myself again and again.

Pastor Brown didn't know how long we had been struggling, but he assured me our life wouldn't always be this way. Either my husband would turn his heart back to us, or he would leave.

I was in enough pain that I was almost okay with either option. I just didn't want to remain in this in-between, not-as-it-should-be life forever.

Where do you find yourself today? In a place of complete uncertainty, a situation that can't continue indefinitely? Struggling with guilt from the past or relief to be able to start over?

I've met single moms from all different situations.

One married to an alcoholic for fifteen years. One never married, living with intense abuse for a decade. Another who lived with an unfaithful husband for years on end.

We come to this place on so many different paths and often have something in common: we are ashamed of our circumstances. I am amazed at how deep this shame can be and how strong its grip is. It's time to face it head-on.

> God never says "tough luck" to those who are in terrible situations. Instead, He says, "Hold on to me."

Let me be totally clear. God never tells women to defend and support a husband who is doing wrong.

Should we build up our husbands honestly? Absolutely. Should we praise their strengths and encourage them in their weaknesses? Every day. Should we keep our disagreements private? Always. Should a woman hide the truth when she is living in neglect or abuse? NEVER.

Yes, you heard me say that. NEVER. If anyone told you that it was your biblical obligation to protect your husband through years of unfaithfulness, neglect, or abuse, I am so sorry. That is not a biblical approach. God never says "tough luck" to those who are in terrible situations.

Instead, He says, "Hold on to me." And if we allow Him to, He will rescue us.

The Beginning of the End

One Saturday, the walls I had kept up for so long finally gave way. The previous several months had been excruciating, and I was fighting with everything in me to save my marriage. My body shook the whole way to Bible study. We met in a beautiful townhouse in the city that day. Soaring ceilings and walls of windows made the space light and airy, in stark contrast to the darkness I felt pressing in on me.

We gathered in the living room, and I sat down on the hardwood floor. Words came tumbling out of my mouth. Tears flowed as I told them what I could of my story. I wasn't ready to face it all yet. To say it out loud. Hearing the words cross my lips made it all the more real. My new friends gathered around me, coming close to my pain, hearing my words, believing me, and insisting that no matter how I felt, I wasn't alone. Letting me know I was safe and loved.

I can't emphasize enough the power of being heard, of telling your story to caring hearts. Elizabeth Murphy, Christian author and speaker, says, "Until you tell your story, it owns you. Once you tell it, you own it, and it loses its power." YES.

I encourage you to find someone trustworthy (a counselor, pastor, dear friend) and tell them your story. Find someone who will walk beside you as you walk through the storm. That changes everything. I left there that day, feeling broken, but strengthened for the journey ahead. I was no longer walking it alone.

There is such beauty in finding others who long to help you carry your burden.

Connections

What part of your story is the hardest to share with others?

First Steps Forward

Who are three compassionate and caring people whom you would consider sharing your story with?

1.

2.

3.

NOT OVER YET

CHAPTER 4

The Rescue

One Sunday afternoon, it all came crashing down. My eyes opened to how much our situation was affecting my daughter and that I couldn't shield her from it anymore. I knew it was time to stand up for us.

Once I had, I shattered. All of the pain of those last few years had built up and finally burst forth. I felt like a glass that had been dropped on cement, scattering shards everywhere. My daughter was napping and I managed to call one friend and my mom. They each heard the absolute panic in my voice and started calling in helpers. My friend, Wendy, called my pastor who assured me I wasn't alone. She then showed up within thirty minutes of my call (no small feat in big city traffic). A herd of wild horses couldn't have kept my mom away. My dad had died several years earlier, so my mom asked me if I wanted her to call my uncle. Absolutely! He called immediately, and I went into a full-on panic attack. I could hear myself talking and couldn't stop.

Words kept falling out of my mouth until my uncle told me to get a glass of water. For future reference, it worked. His seemingly odd request snapped me out of whatever was misfiring in my brain. He patiently waited while I got a glass of water and took a drink. Then he reminded me to breathe and told me what to do that first night. I had no idea. My brain couldn't make any decisions, and his perspective was completely level-headed.

He sent my cousin and her husband to be with me, and their very presence made me feel safer. I had no shortage of people surrounding me, and all of them played a part in walking me through those first hours. I am eternally grateful. Their presence made such a difference for me.

Over the next several months, my daughter and I spent a lot of time at my sister's house, which became my sanctuary. I spent so many hours on her sofa, crying over the loss of my marriage, my plans, my dreams. Everything I thought my life would be. My sister patiently, lovingly sat and listened, witnessing each tear. She held space for my grief. I don't know how she listened to the same unanswerable questions over and over and sat there with such compassion. I only know God used her to carry me through those days.

Those who will sit with you through your pain, who will listen without judgment, are priceless.

If I could share any piece of inspiration with you, it would be this: don't count people out. There may have been distance and disconnection because of your situation, but your friends and family might be at home praying for the day you'll let them in. They may have seen the cracks in your armor that you try so desperately to cover. And they may be ready to jump at a moment's notice and run to your side.

I am praying that's how it would be for you. If you find yourself in a situation that is scary or unsafe, please ask for help. I am praying that God will send exactly the people you need in that moment so that you will feel and truly be safe.

If you don't have those people in your life, if the people you know are not safe, strong people who love you and will walk with you through life, find new people. Call a women's shelter, join a single moms' group at a local church, find a group online, or join a Bible study with other women. It will take work to build new friendships, and it will absolutely be worth it. And no matter what, remember that God is right there with you all the time. You may not have friends and family at the ready, but you have God. He really is all we need.

Our Deliverer

Those first days and months are not easy, but you will create your new normal. It probably won't look anything like your life before, but you and God can create it together. Lean into Him. His promises are trustworthy and true. Ask Him for wisdom for your future, one step at a time, and remember our God is the God of redemption. Not only redemption from sin but also redemption from the pits and distress we find ourselves in.

Psalm 107 sums this up so beautifully; four times in this chapter alone: "Then they cried to the Lord in their trouble, and he delivered them from their distress."

Some of the people in Psalm 107 got into distress on their own, sometimes it was external things that happened to them, but the result was always the same. The people of God were in trouble: in chains, hopeless, in darkness, wasting away. And God's actions were the same every time. When they cried out to Him, He rescued them.

He rescued them! He satisfied the longing soul. He brought them out of darkness and burst their chains apart. He healed them and delivered them. He told the storms to be still and hushed the waves of the sea.

These are His promises to you and to me. They are still true today. When we cry out to Him, He will rescue us from our distress. The rescue will look different for all of us. Some husbands will turn back to their wives, some husbands will leave, and some women will leave and find a safe place. Whatever happens, God will be your strength and will not leave you alone. No matter what your rescue looks like, He will take care of you.

> He holds your future in the hands that created the stars.

I wish I could show you your future so you could take a fresh breath of hope. But I can point you to our God, who is our hope. He holds your future in the hands that created the stars. He has plans for you even when you can't see them. If God allows your marriage to end, He will carry you through it. Hold on. It's not over yet. And if you are too tired to hold on, reach out your hand.

He will hold onto you.

Connections

What is holding you back from asking for a rescue?

First Step Forward

Write a prayer to God asking Him to rescue you from a specific struggle you are facing.

_____

_____

_____

_____

_____

NOT OVER YET

CHAPTER 5

The Broken Mug

After years of concealing my everyday life, the habit was difficult to break. Even when it was clear to everyone else that it had all fallen apart, I was fighting like a madwoman to hold my life together. I was going to muscle through life by sheer force of will, if needed. Or so I thought.

Those first few months after my ex-husband left were such a blur, each day looking much like the next. The grief was overwhelming, and I didn't have a break. There was no one to watch my daughter, so I could take a bath, or a nap, or go to Target by myself.

But, every Sunday, no matter how I felt, I went to church. And I cried. I cried through every service. It was humiliating, but I couldn't help it. A dam had burst. Now that I couldn't hide my failing marriage or the pain I was in anymore, it flowed out constantly.

I believed that God was still trustworthy. I believed that He had a plan. I just didn't want His plan. I wanted my plan. I wanted my husband to want us again and come home. I wanted the dream I would never have.

I will never forget the day I finally let go.

I was once again crying out to God with my heart broken open, hopeless. I didn't know what to do next or how to possibly turn our life around. By then, we had moved in with my mom and were still struggling to get by financially. I couldn't see past that day, that moment. I couldn't imagine a future of hope and joy. I thought maybe there would always be struggle.

But that day, sitting on the floor next to my bed, once again crying out to God, He gave me a vision.

I saw my hands holding a shattered mug. It had cracks all over it, and it took both of my hands to hold it together, and even so, water was running out everywhere. No matter how much I tried, I couldn't fix it. I couldn't hold it together with my bare hands, no matter how stubborn I was and how much I wouldn't give up. He nudged my heart and told me to let go. To let the mug fall and be broken, which it was anyway. To trust Him to pick it up and make something beautiful from the shattered pieces.

That was the day our world turned—the day I started moving forward to a new life instead of desperately trying to hold onto the life I had lost. That was the day I finally accepted God's plan instead of insisting on my own.

I put shoes on my faith and chose to live it out—trusting that He could see so much more than I could (He can) and that He will work everything together for my good and His glory (He will).

If you are trying to hold it all together, to put on a happy face for the watching world, maybe it's time for you to let go. To admit that life feels impossible right now. To admit that you can't hold it together by yourself. To admit that you need help. God is waiting, just waiting for you to let Him in, to let Him do what only He can do and pull you up out of the pit.

Our God is the God of hopeless cases. Only they aren't so hopeless to Him.

He Will Make a Way

Imagine the Israelites up against the Red Sea. Their life had been hard. Their entire race had been enslaved for generations in Egypt, and they had just been through the most amazing, dramatic rescue in history.

They had witnessed the ten plagues on Egypt, the final one being the death of the firstborn of every Egyptian family. Then the Egyptians gave all their treasure to the Israelites as the Israelites headed out of town. I imagine they were celebrating 200 years of slavery brought to an astonishing end, the first time any of these generations living had experienced freedom. They barely got their journey underway when their captors changed their minds and chased them down.

One minute, they were filled with jubilation, and the next, they found themselves cornered between a sea and the Egyptian army. They were out of options with nowhere to go. There was no path ahead of them, and they were certain their lives were over.

That sounds so familiar to me.

When we begin this journey of being single moms, we are often in positions like the Israelites: leaving a bad situation while not being able to even imagine a path ahead, let alone see one—wondering if the next minute is going to be the one that does us in.

If that's what you're feeling, hold on.

God hasn't failed us yet, and He doesn't plan to start now. Check out what He did for the Israelites.

As they heard the Egyptian army closing in, hooves pounding and chariot wheels bouncing over dry ground, they panicked and asked Moses why he had brought them out of slavery to have them die now.

Even after seeing all the miracles God performed in the process of their rescue, they were still full of fear. When Moses faced the sea and raised his hands up, I bet some of them thought he had lost his mind. Then they watched as God pushed the sea back to the right and to the left and made a clear, dry path for them to cross over. It was a rescue they didn't see coming. A path where none had been. A solution that never would have entered their minds.

> The God who sees it all and holds it all isn't afraid of any of it.

The God who did that is fully capable of protecting you and me, too. He created a way for them, and He can create a way for you. He created this world, and He controls all of it. He can bend all of creation to His will anytime He wants to.

Hopeless cases don't scare Him. They are only hopeless to us because of our human perspective. The God who sees it all and holds it all isn't afraid of any of it.

I love this quote from Pastor Louie Giglio: "God is not intimidated by the odds. He's like, DUDE, I've made galaxies."

YES! He is a God who sees not only the possibilities of the future but actually knows how they will play out. He knows how He is going to use this to sanctify you and glorify Himself. He knows how He will use this to point others to Christ. He knows it all.

That is the God who loves you. The God who knows it all and controls it all. The God who sees it all and can use it all. The God who can make a vertical wall out of water whenever He wants. He will not let you fall. If you depend on Him, if you trust Him, if you give it all to Him, He will carry you.

Connections

What dream are you holding onto that God is asking
you to let go of? What good things might
happen if you let it go?

First Step Forward

Write down three times (no matter how big or small they
seem) when you have seen God move in your life.

1.

2.

3.

NOT OVER YET

CHAPTER 6

Get Up!

Once we have let go of what will never be and turned to God, asking for His redeeming hand, it's time to start building that new life. The grief wants to keep us down. And so does the enemy. Satan wants nothing more than to see us stuck in the past, pressed down by the grief.

I remember the many months before the end of my marriage that had taken every ounce of my strength and the feeling that I would be trapped in that agonizing life forever.

I remember the days of not wanting to get out of bed, of dragging my exhausted body, bit by bit out from under the safety and security of the covers, until a toe finally touched the floor.

I remember hearing my daughter awaken across the hall and sighing, wondering how I was going to do it all again. And I remember pushing through with God's strength. Asking Him to help me do it all again, day after exhausting day.

I had a choice to make, and so do you. You can stay stuck in the pain, trapped in the fear, held tight by debilitating memories. Or you can choose hope. Fight for a better future. Choose to let the past go and look with hope toward a better time.

You get to choose to build an amazing future for yourself and your children.

Maybe you're feeling stuck right now and unable to see any hope for the future. Maybe your spirit is so trampled that you want to stay under the blankets forever.

I get it. I really do. And I'm going to be your bossy big sister for a minute.

Get up

Get out of that bed or off that sofa and get moving again. Your children need you, and you deserve a great, big, beautiful life. In fact, not only do you deserve it, you were created for it. You were created to love and be loved, to see the beauty of creation that God made so you could enjoy it, to join life again, and hear your children's laughter once more. To laugh with them.

What are your hopes and dreams for the future? Can you see that far? Can you imagine beauty in the life you can create for yourself and your kiddos? I can. I can see it because I have lived it, and I will tell you it is absolutely worth fighting for. That amazing future is worth every breath you have and every ounce of your energy. Keep getting up. Keep loving those little ones. Keep holding on. The future isn't going to build itself.

Your children need you. You are now their biggest defender. They are counting on you to stand up for them. Sure, some divorces are amicable, and the kids go between homes easily. If both parents are trustworthy and care for the children well, that's amazing! Not every child of divorced parents needs physical protection. But those that do need it desperately.

I have watched parents crumble at the abuse their kids receive when they are in the other home. I have watched single moms who were worn out allow their children to go into homes where they were in physical danger simply because they desperately needed a break. And I have watched moms fight with everything in them to protect their children from those same dangers. The younger our kids are, the more vulnerable they are —physically and emotionally. It is our job to protect their bodies and hearts.

"Above all else, guard your heart, for everything you do flows from it." (Proverbs 4:23)

We need to protect our hearts, guard our hearts, keep our hearts from being hurt or changed or damaged by others. And when our kids are little, it's our job to protect theirs, too. If you are exhausted and don't have family or friends who can help, find a church or a women's center. There are places that will give respite care for your

> Keep getting up. Keep loving those little ones. Keep holding on. The future isn't going to build itself.

children so you can take a breath. You may be exhausted from the fight. Don't give up. Your children are counting on you to protect them and keep your family going.

The best practical advice I can possibly give you if you are in your own tsunami of tears is to just do the next thing, whatever that is.

Does your child need breakfast? Dry Cheerios are perfectly acceptable. Is there anything clean to wear? If not, do one load of laundry.

Don't look at the piles of dirty clothes and the dishes in the sink and the future filled with uncertainty. Simply do the next thing. And little by little, you'll be able to see further down the path.

Be the mom who gets back up. Day after day.
Be the mom who looks to the future. Day after day.
Be the mom who chooses hope. Day after day.

Connections
What time of day is hardest or most discouraging for you?
What can you do to change that?

First Step Forward
Write down three things you can do every day
that bring you joy.

1.

2.

3.

CHAPTER 7

The Fight for Forgiveness

I wish I could tell you that forgiveness came easily and quickly for me. I wish I could tell you that I followed God's will and instantly forgave my ex-husband.

I did not.

It took me several years to reach that point. Forgiveness is not easy, but it is absolutely worth fighting for.

After a couple of years, God softened my heart enough that I wanted to want to forgive. Yes, you read that right. I wasn't ready to forgive, and I didn't want to forgive, but I did want to be obedient to God, which meant forgiving. I literally began praying, "Lord, please make me want to forgive. I want to follow Your will, and I really don't feel it, so please make me want to forgive."

I prayed that for months and months, willing my heart to change but not feeling it change. I repeated my prayer over and over, sometimes feeling that I was failing God by not forgiving. God clearly tells us to forgive, and here I was, not even close to forgiving.

Each time my daughter had a reaction to her loss, each time I got another bill I couldn't pay, each time another moment of pain shook me, my heart began to race, my face felt flushed, and the anger rose inside me once again. I kept asking for forgiveness for my anger and praying for the ability to forgive. I wondered if I would ever be able to.

God softened my heart little by little, chipping away at the walls I had built to protect myself. My prayer became an actual request that He would help me forgive. I finally wanted to but still couldn't do it on my own.

Again, I prayed for months, frustrated with myself that I couldn't do it. God in His great grace could forgive my every sin, and I couldn't forgive this? The guilt was painful.

And then it happened.

I felt the Holy Spirit's nudge again. And this time, everything stopped. The Holy Spirit impressed on my heart that by not forgiving, I was saying that my Savior's death on the cross wasn't enough to cover these sins—my Savior, who was betrayed, beaten, mocked, and hung on a cross for the sins of the entire world. For the sin of every single person who will come to Him and accept the forgiveness that He died to offer.

My Savior's sacrifice, not enough to cover this sin? Unthinkable. Who am I to hold anything against anyone when my Savior already died for that sin? How little did I think of His sacrifice for us all?

And in that moment, forgiveness washed over me and poured out from me. I was overwhelmed with peace that filled me to the brim and spilled over. I asked God to forgive me for my unforgiveness, for minimizing His sacrifice.

I told Him how incredibly grateful I was that He had moved my heart enough to forgive. I am so thankful God is patient with us. He didn't hit me over the head with what I needed to do. He waited and worked for so long, never giving up on me. And now, according to Psalm 103:12, my sin of unforgiveness is removed from me as far as the east is from the west.

Gone. Forgotten. Never to be remembered again. I can hardly contain the joy that comes from that knowledge!

In the days that followed, I found myself passionately praying for my ex-husband and his new wife. It was a change in my heart that I never saw coming, and truly, only God could have made happen. God drew me to my knees in worship for His forgiveness of me and in my desire to pray for them.

When we forgive someone, the responsibility of their sin isn't taken from them. Jesus died for the sins of everyone who will repent and ask Him for forgiveness, in all history and all of the future. Our forgiveness doesn't change the need for someone to repent to Him. It takes all the bitterness and anger out of our hearts and makes us more like Jesus.

If you are struggling with forgiveness, I want you to know the battle to forgive is worth every tear slipping down your cheek, every argument in your mind, every ounce of struggle in your heart. Unforgiveness hardens our hearts and does nothing to the one we aren't forgiving. Unforgiveness will never show

> God drew me to my knees in worship for His forgiveness of me and in my desire to pray for them.

them Christ's love or allow us to live in the freedom he offers. Forgiveness isn't saying that their actions didn't matter. Forgiveness means we aren't responsible for giving them their consequences. That's God's job. We're simply giving it back to Him. Once we do, we are free to live our lives without carrying that burden around with us.

Forgiveness vs. Reconciliation

Forgiveness is hard enough when someone says something terrible to hurt you. If you have lived with actual abuse or have seen your children hurt, it's harder still, and it may be wisest to walk away and protect yourself and your children while still fighting to forgive. In that situation, forgiveness might feel impossible to you. But it's not impossible for God. He can move your heart to forgive and still protect your heart moving forward.

Please don't miss this crucial piece: forgiveness and reconciliation are not the same. While forgiveness depends entirely on you, reconciliation requires something from both parties. Forgiveness is you not being responsible for their consequences, not holding their sin against them. It does not require that they are sorry or even acknowledge their wrongdoing. Forgiveness is required of us by God.

Reconciliation involves sincere repentance met with forgiveness. It involves turning away from sin and then lots of time and counseling to work through the past and build a relationship for the future. Whether it's a friendship that works for your situation or a full reconciliation of your marriage is up to you, your ex, and God. Please get wise counsel to help you work through these possibilities. It's easy to have our judgment clouded by our past experiences, and this is not a decision to go into lightly or quickly.

Connections

What sin has someone committed against you that you can't seem to let go of? Is your continuing anger towards them affecting your life and relationships with others? Are you striving for forgiveness or reconciliation?

First Steps Forward

Consider your own sins that Christ has forgiven by His sacrificial death. If you are struggling with forgiveness, write a prayer asking God to help you.

_____

_____

_____

_____

_____

NOT OVER YET

CHAPTER 8

Give God Your Pain

OK. I know this sounds crazy. Really crazy. And it might not make sense to you for a while, but please hear me out.

There is so much pain involved in the breakdown of a marriage. Maybe you were hurt by unfaithfulness, physical abuse, emotional abuse, or seeing your children hurt or neglected. Whether your marriage ended suddenly or you fought for it for many years, the pain is intense. The smallest things can trigger memories; even good memories of special times you had with your spouse or as a family remind you of all that you lost. Bad memories of hurts, disappointments, abuse remind you of all that you lived through. These triggers can be everywhere. A word…the cover of a book…an expression. I continue to be amazed at what can trigger a memory. Recently for me, it was the death of a famous actor. My ex-husband and I saw him live on stage twice. The first time was early in our marriage, and that experience literally changed the course of our lives. The second time was years later, a rare occasion when we went out together —one of the few highlights during a very dark time. The death of this actor brought it all back to me.

In the early days after my ex-husband left, the pain was intense. And for a few years, the pain would seize me many times a day, surprising me when I least expected it. My daughter and I would be having a great time out on an adventure and I would see a family all together. Mom, dad, kids. Suddenly, I would feel that jab of pain that my daughter and I didn't have that anymore. Once I spied a child sitting happily on her dad's shoulders at a parade and I remembered watching my daughter do the same.

And then I reached another turning point. It started slowly, with an idea that I didn't believe at all, planted in my head during a women's Bible study at church on a Wednesday night. I don't remember what we were studying that night, but the leader was someone whose faith and biblical knowledge I admired. Someone I would go to seeking wisdom, certain she would never steer me wrong. During this meeting, she was talking about sacrifice, saying that a sacrifice we could make for God is to give Him our pain.

Excuse me? I literally scoffed. Then I quickly tried to cover it with a cough.

Now, I don't typically do that in a Bible study. Like ever. I am a rule follower. If I ever disagree with a Bible study leader, I search for the biblical answer on my own. Maybe once in a great while, I will say what I believe to be correct if it's appropriate. But my reaction was so strong. The idea of giving my pain to God and having it be a sacrifice I could make that would honor Him was completely ridiculous to me. Absurd. It made no sense. The God of the universe is so far beyond all I can imagine, so great and amazing that He deserves all my praise. He deserves glory and honor and worship and obedience. Not my pain.

I decided to ignore what she said. I didn't believe it and couldn't see how it could be biblical, so I decided to forget it.

God had a different plan.

The thought kept coming back to me for weeks on end. "Give Him your pain" kept floating through my mind at the weirdest times.

A couple of months after that night in Bible study, I was looking in the mirror, frustrated with hearing that phrase again. The pain was still fierce, and I didn't know how to lay it down. I finally told God in no uncertain terms, I didn't want the pain anymore, and I didn't know how to give it to Him. If He wanted it, He was going to have to take it from me.

And He did.

At that moment, I was overwhelmed with peace and felt incredible relief physically, as if I had been carrying around fifty-pound weights that were hanging on a yoke around my neck and then suddenly were gone. I had been carrying it for so long that I didn't even know how heavy it had become until He lifted it away.

As the days went on, I felt so much freedom. I was free to feel more joy. I was free to serve Him more fully. I was free to become who He created me to be.

> As the days went on, I felt so much freedom. I was free to become who He created me to be.

Looking back, I can see the change clearly as I let the pain go and made room to find new joy. I see a reflection of it in my life as a mom. When my children are hurting, I will do anything to take that pain from them. If I could carry it for them and relieve them of the pain, it would actually bring me joy.

Maybe that's how it was with God and me. Maybe He loves me so much that He wants me to be free to live in the joy He created for me. Maybe He wants me to live free from the constant pain. Maybe He loves me enough and is strong enough to handle my pain, so I don't have to. Maybe He is strong enough to carry yours.

Life is still hard. God told us it would be. There may always be moments and memories that make us sad. But the pain is so much less, and the joy is so much more once we know where to take the pain when it comes. When we see how much God wants us to live a joy-filled life, overflowing with His abundant grace and mercy.

His willingness, even eagerness, to take on our sin, to take on our pain, to take on our struggles, and carry them for us is overwhelming. We never have to be alone, never have to carry our burdens on our own. God is right there waiting for us to set down our burdens and let Him lighten our load.

Connections

Is there pain you're holding onto that you can't seem to put down? How would life be better if you were free from that pain? Ask God to take your pain so you can live in the freedom He provides.

First Steps Forward

List three areas of your life where you want joy to replace the pain.

1.

2.

3.

NOT OVER YET

CHAPTER 9

You + God Are Enough

I've heard the horror stories. I've seen the statistics about children raised by single parents. I was personally told that my daughter was at a disadvantage because she has a single mom.

And yet, there are so many stories in the Bible that prove otherwise. God doesn't say He will only provide for children in two-parent homes. He doesn't say He will only bless children whose parents are still married. God doesn't write us off, so why do we?

Look at Paul's comments about Timothy and the influence of his mother and grandmother. "I am reminded of your sincere faith, which first lived in your grandmother Lois and in your mother Eunice and, I am persuaded, now lives in you also" (2 Timothy 1:5). There is no mention of a dad. We don't know if a dad was present, but his influence wasn't noted. The mother's and grandmother's were.

How about Hagar in the wilderness? She had been used, mistreated, and eventually cast out. She and her son were on their own in the desert of Beersheba. They ran out of food and water, and Hagar gave up. She left her son under a bush and walked away because she couldn't bear to watch him die. Then an angel of God told her not to be afraid and that God would make her son into a great nation. God saw her when the world didn't, and He rescued her and her son. She called Him "The God Who Sees" (Genesis 16:13).

Then there's the widow in 1 Kings 17. She had a handful of flour and a bit of oil left, and was preparing to make one last meal for herself and her son. Again, God had other plans. He sent Elijah to her and asked her to feed him. She was faithful and did as God asked her in spite of only having enough left for one meal. From the day of her obedience until the day the famine ended, God kept her supplies of flour and oil from running out. She was able to keep feeding her family purely by the grace of God.

> They all had exactly what they needed, simply because God said so.

Do you see the connection, the thread that runs through each of these stories and our own? Human need is followed by God's presence and provision. He responds to our needs. He is present with us always. He provides for His children.

God was alive and well in Timothy's household. God was with Hagar and Ishmael in the desert. He provided miraculously for the widow and her son. They all had exactly what they needed, simply because God said so.

I wonder what He's going to do for you and me. I wonder if a jar of peanut butter will never run out. I wonder if He will send an angel (or an angel disguised as a friend) to remind us of His provision and protection. I wonder what lengths He will go to so we know He is always for us.

It's beyond our imaginations, and every time He provides, I am surprised. I should be expecting it by now, but God's goodness never ceases to amaze me. When I'm sad, He provides comfort. When my girls are struggling, He provides wisdom so I can guide them well. When I'm lonely, He is close at hand.

I know that God is with us every single day. I know that He is always present, and we are the ones who get busy and don't keep up the conversation. I try to remember to talk to Him throughout my day, not only in concentrated times of prayer.

Anytime something comes up that we wish we could talk to a husband about, we can take it right to God. Whether it's about work or parenting or hard times or victories, He wants to be a part of it all. He wants us to share our lives with Him. He created us to be in relationship with others and with Him.

There are still going to be moments of loneliness where we wish for an actual hand to hold and an audible voice to hear. But times of sharing all that we are and all that we have with Jesus are so very sweet and refreshing and joyful.

I know that my girls have some things missing in their lives—a male perspective. A man who can tell them they are wonderful and loved. A man to help support us, protect us, laugh with us, comfort us. Sometimes I really wish they had a full-time mom and a full-time dad, both of whom adore them and are their biggest fans. But I refuse to believe that my daughters are doomed to become a statistic because of the lack of a father in our home.

I fully believe that God will make up for what I lack. And the more I lean into Him, the more my daughters will see Him in me, see Him reflected in my life, see Him as everything I (and they) need. "God, whatever I have messed up today, please fix it and fill it up and make it right." I am only human, and He knows that.

As Pastor Matt Chandler points out, "Throughout the Bible, it seems like God has a special ear for mamas crying out for their babies. Where the ideal is lacking, grace abounds."

God is ready and willing to do what our kids need. To give us the strength to overcome whatever we face as single parents leading our families alone.

Connections
What is your biggest fear for your children? What do you lack that you can ask God to make up for?

First Step Forward
List three areas in which you will trust God to be the other parent in your home.

1.

2.

3.

CHAPTER 10

Praying Over Your Children

One of the best commitments we can make to our children is to pray for them continually. I pray specific verses for and over my girls. What a privilege it is to learn their strengths and challenges and to pray for God to show Himself in their lives.

How many times did I sit over a toddler bed praying these precious words over a precious heart? Now I want to pray over both of my girls while they are listening. Let them hear the treasured words about the amazing love God has for them.

Pray for them to be rooted and established in Christ.

There is nothing more important we could pray for them. Nothing. Our children need to know where to go when times get tough. They need to know where to go when they don't have the answers. They need to know God goes before them and is constantly with them. They need to learn to turn to Him for help and comfort. When they are no longer under my roof, I pray that they will always turn to God first. When I pray for this, I especially love praying Scripture over my girls. Anywhere "you" or "your" appears, I replace it with their name.

"For this reason, I kneel before the Father, from whom every family in heaven and on earth derives its name. I pray that out of his glorious riches, he may strengthen you with power through his Spirit in your inner being so that Christ may dwell in your hearts through faith. And I pray that you, being rooted and established in love, may have power, together with all the Lord's holy people, to grasp how wide and long and high and deep is the love of Christ, and to know this love that surpasses knowledge—that you may be filled to the measure of all the fullness of God. Now to him who is able to do immeasurably more than all we ask or imagine, according to his power that is at work within us, to him be glory in the church and in Christ Jesus throughout all generations, for ever and ever! Amen." (Ephesians 3:14-21).

"So then, just as you received Christ Jesus as Lord, continue to live your lives in him, rooted and built up in him, strengthened in the faith as you were taught, and overflowing with thankfulness." (Colossians 2:6-7).

Pray that they will stay in God and bear much fruit

One of my greatest desires is to know my children are following Christ. I want them to live set apart as reflections of God in this world. I want them to know joy and hope throughout their lives. Joy and hope that are unique and immeasurable and supplied solely by faith in God. They will make their own choices in life, some good and some bad, and I will spend all of my breath asking God to pull them close.

"I am the vine; you are the branches. If you remain in me and I in you, you will bear much fruit; apart from me, you can do nothing" (John 15:5).

"For this reason, since the day we heard about you, we have not stopped praying for you. We continually ask God to fill you with the knowledge of his will through all the wisdom and understanding that the Spirit gives, so that you may live a life worthy of the Lord and please him in every way: bearing fruit in every good work, growing in the knowledge of God" (Colossians 1:9-10).

Pray for God to send Christian men into their lives to speak His truth over them

Maybe this will be a teacher, a leader at church, an uncle, or a grandfather. You may have no idea who it will be. It doesn't matter. Lay it at Jesus' feet. Tell Him of the need and watch Him provide. He said to let the children come to Him. I believe He takes great joy in helping them find Him. I'm praying for my girls to see men who run hard after God, who have seen Him work in their lives and have the passion for teaching the next generation to follow hard after God, too.

"Since my youth, God, you have taught me, and to this day, I declare your marvelous deeds. Even when I am old and gray, do not forsake me, my God, till I declare your power to the next generation, your mighty acts to all who are to come" (Psalm 71:17-18).

"And what you have heard from me in the presence of many witnesses entrust to faithful men, who will be able to teach others also" (2 Timothy 2:2 ESV).

Pray for abundant examples of godly marriages

As a single mom, I can't show my children what a godly marriage looks like firsthand. I can't show them how a man should treat a woman. I don't want my children settling for less because they don't know what to look for. I am so grateful for the time we get to spend with couples who live out their marriage vows and love each other well.

These times can be hard to come by for a single mom. I find there are so many other single moms, other women in our lives, which is beautiful. But there are very few men. When an event comes up, and my girls have the opportunity to be around Christian families and Christian couples, we are all in.

Afterward, I talk to my girls about what I saw. If a husband treated his wife well, you better believe I noticed it and will be pointing it out later. I want them to see what pure love looks like. If we get to see a couple disagree and do so lovingly, I may as well have won the jackpot! What an amazing lesson that is for my children!

> "Husbands, love your wives, just as Christ loved the church and gave himself up for her to make her holy, cleansing her by the washing with water through the word, and to present her to himself as a radiant church, without stain or wrinkle or any other blemish, but holy and blameless. In this same way, husbands ought to love their wives as their own bodies. He who loves his wife loves himself.

After all, no one ever hated their own body, but they feed and care for their body, just as Christ does the church— for we are members of his body. "For this reason, a man will leave his father and mother and be united to his wife, and the two will become one flesh." This is a profound mystery— but I am talking about Christ and the church. However, each one of you also must love his wife as he loves himself, and the wife must respect her husband." (Ephesians 5:25-33).

"Be completely humble and gentle; be patient, bearing with one another in love." (Ephesians 4:2).

Pray that they use their spiritual gifts

We all have unique gifts and abilities that God designed us with. He planned ahead of time many good works for us to do with our gifts. Our children need to know that. They need to learn to see their gifts and understand how much the world needs them. They need to know that God created them on purpose for a purpose. They are invaluable in God's eyes and can accomplish much for Him, no matter how young or old they are.

"Don't let anyone look down on you because you are young, but set an example for the believers in speech, in conduct, in love, in faith, and in purity. Do not neglect your gift" (I Timothy 4:12, 14).

"We have different gifts, according to the grace given to each of us. If your gift is prophesying, then prophesy in accordance with your faith; if it is serving, then serve; if it is teaching, then teach;

if it is to encourage, then give encouragement; if it is giving, then give generously; if it is to lead, do it diligently; if it is to show mercy, do it cheerfully" (Romans 12:6-8).

Pray that they seek God's shelter in the storms they face

So often, our responses to the struggles of life determine our future. I've seen people walk completely away from God, and I've seen people run towards God. I want my children to be the ones that run to God, knowing He is their safe place, their refuge, their constant help.

"But let all who take refuge in You be glad; let them ever sing for joy. Spread your protection over them, that those who love your name may rejoice in you." (Psalm 5:11).

"The LORD is a refuge for the oppressed, a stronghold in times of trouble." (Psalm 9:9).

I want my children to know God and follow Him every day of their lives. I want them to know their value is in Him and that He will always protect them and provide for them. That a relationship with Christ is worth more than anything they could gain in this world. My desire is that my children shine His light everywhere they go. For that, I will pray as long as I have breath.

Connections

What gifts do your children have that you can pray for God to use? What weaknesses do your children have that you can pray for protection over?

First Step Forward

Write out three specific areas to pray about for your children.

1.

2.

3.

NOT OVER YET

CHAPTER 11

Set Down Your Pride

I recently spoke with a friend of mine who has a doctorate from a seminary, is married, and works in full-time ministry where she encounters plenty of single moms. In her ministry, she noticed that single moms find it very hard to ask for help and she wanted to know why. I told her part of it is pride.

It's one thing to be in need for a short time, from the loss of a job, illness, etc. As single moms, some of us are in need for years on end. No one wants to ask for help over and over. Many of us find it hard to even accept help when it's offered. We want to feel like we can do it all on our own, show our kids how tough we are.

Sometimes the question itself is the problem. What do you need? Seriously? We need everything. We need food and school supplies, and the kids wrecked their new shoes, and the rent is due, and the sink won't drain, and we're out of toilet paper. Right?

There are so many needs that when someone asks what they can do, sometimes we don't know where to start. Sometimes the needs seem insurmountable, and we feel bad placing them on anyone else's shoulders.

But here I am, telling you to ask for help, no matter how you feel.

We often want to power through every obstacle alone. And I know that isn't God's plan. He created us for relationship so we would take care of each other. He designed us each with special gifts and skills and He wants us to come together to get things done.

The original church in Acts went so far as to sell all they had every seven years and put all the money together and split it up, so everyone had the same. That's much more extreme than asking for help around the house.

Try flipping the scene around. If your friend or someone you know was in need, would you want to help them? Of course, you would! Would you be upset that they asked? I doubt it. So why do we think others will be frustrated if we ask? Let the past go. Let your pride go. God did not create you to take everything on by yourself. He doesn't expect you to raise the children, bring home the money, fix the car, install a new dishwasher, and never sleep.

He knows you. He created you.

He is not surprised by the situation you find yourself in, and He wants to help. He already has a plan for how to fix the dishwasher or get the kiddos to basketball practice. That plan often involves us taking a deep breath and asking someone for help.

The Great Christmas Tree Fiasco

It was the very first Christmas that my daughter and I lived on our own after her dad left. I was desperate to make good memories with her, no matter what.

I thought cutting our own Christmas tree would be a grand adventure. I found a Christmas tree farm, and off we went. We searched through the rows of trees, trying them out by standing next to them to check height, looking from every angle to see if the tree was full all over. We found our perfect tree. I decided to cut it down.

Yes, they had precut trees. Yes, the people who owned the tree farm would have cut it for me. But I wanted to do it. I wanted to prove that I could. I wanted my daughter to see that her mom was strong and tough and could handle anything.

I laid down on my side, under the tree, with a slightly rusted manual handsaw.

Back and forth, back and forth. Barely a mark. Back and forth, back and forth some more. Sweating now, but only about a quarter of an inch of cut. Back and forth, back and forth.

After about fifteen minutes, I stood up for a break, the blood rushing from my head. My daughter was bored and pretty sure we would never go home, that I would be lying on the ground cutting the Christmas tree until Easter.

Then I saw him: A strong-looking guy in his twenties, with his family a few rows over, was headed our way. Apparently, while I was trying to be strong and tough, others noticed that I was getting nowhere.

He walked over and asked if he could cut the tree for me, to which I said yes. He moved in with his power saw, and ten seconds later, the tree was cut, and we were heading home.

If I hadn't let that nice twenty-something guy cut our tree, I would still be under there, sawing away. We never would have gotten the tree home and found out our eyes had been bigger than our living room, and the top of the tree bent against the ceiling.

We would never have heard the tree stand snap or lurched to catch the tree as it fell. We never would have leaned it against the wall and headed to the thrift store for a new-to-us tree stand (that we still use today!). We would never have seen our crocheted angel bending over on top of the tree as she was pushed up against the ceiling. And we wouldn't have had this family story that we will talk and laugh about forever.

I wanted to teach my daughter I was strong enough to handle everything on my own. I realized she needed to learn to ask for help when she needed it.

By the way, other people need help, too. Married or not, every mom needs help at some point. Lay it all down and be willing to ask. And if someone says no? Don't take it personally. There are things you need to say no to as well. Things you can't take on right now. It's OK. Maybe that family is overwhelmed, too. Find someone else you can ask.

> He's been providing for single moms since the beginning of time, and He's not about to stop now.

Last year, I got incredibly sick for about two weeks. Nothing was getting done except for getting my girls to school. I'm still not sure how I managed to drive them every day, but somehow, I got them to school and back—nothing else. No laundry. No dishes. No cooking. I didn't tell people how sick I was, and I didn't ask for help. But one of my friends figured it out.

She showed up one day with a Costco chicken pot pie in hand and proceeded to wash all my dishes while I slouched in a chair in the kitchen. I was literally too sick to protest. She gave me an incredible gift that day. Not asking what I needed, not asking permission to do something, she just jumped in and took care of us.

All I had to do was open the door.

The next time someone asks if you need help, do your best to say yes. Or if someone says they are going to drop something off for you, for Heaven's sake, don't act like you don't need it. Put down your pride and say thank you.

Time and time again, God has provided exactly what we needed right when we needed it. He's been providing for single moms since the beginning of time, and He's not about to stop now. Lay all of your worries at His feet. I promise you He can handle them, and He already has them covered. "Your Father knows what you need before you ask Him" (Matthew 6:8).

Connections

What is one project around your house you need help with? Ask God for provision, and be ready to accept help, no matter how He delivers it.

First Step Forward

List three people or organizations you could call for help.

1.

2.

3.

NOT OVER YET

CHAPTER 12

Set Yourself Up for Success

We need to be intentional about helping our families thrive. This isn't the time to let it all go, even though we may feel like it daily. A great big, beautiful life for us and our children won't happen on its own. We need to take concrete steps that lead us there, and we don't have to walk the journey alone. There are amazing people out there waiting to love us well and help carry our burdens.

Church

Get involved in a church if you aren't already. Find a Bible-believing church that is living as God intended, is vibrant and active, and truly cares for each other. Church was meant to be a place where we can soak in God's truth and be surrounded by people who know and love God. This is how God designed it. He gifted each person with what they need to do the works He planned for them (yes, that means you, too!).

And the Bible frequently calls believers to work together as His church. "Rather, speaking the truth in love, we are to grow up in every way into him who is the head, into Christ from whom the whole body, joined and held together by every joint with which it is equipped, when each part is working properly, makes the body grow so that it builds itself up in love." (Ephesians 4:15-16 ESV).

When we moved closer to my family, I had to leave my beloved little church that had walked through my hardest days with me. I tried church after church (again). I found one that preached from the Bible, had music I loved to worship with, and most of all, had an amazing program for kids.

On my third Sunday there, the pastor of the middle and high school groups spoke during the service about their program. He talked about preparing the kids so well that by the time they walked out those doors after high school, they would be ready to shine God's light to the world and stand in their faith no matter what life threw at them. I didn't need to hear anything else. That's what I wanted and what we needed: Believers who would pour their lives into my daughter's life and be additional guiding voices for her.

The youth group has amazing leaders who love my girls so well and call them higher. They help my girls see who God created them to be, how they are wired, and what their gifts are. These relationships are helping form my girls into who they will be as adults. These men and women work right alongside me to build solid foundations in my girls' hearts and lives. Foundations they can lean on to carry them through every hardship life will bring.

Find your People

Often in the process of becoming a single mom, we lose some friends. Whether it's through a divorce, break-up, or entering a new stage of life that others don't understand, our friendships change.

We all need people to live this life with, and sometimes we have to work hard to find and build those friendships.

My isolation during my marriage made me feel very alone. I don't want to live that way ever again, so I work hard to see old friends when I can and find new friends when possible. My best friend lives four states away, and I craved connection in person, so I prayed for years for another Christian friend. God has provided several women I can depend on and support; godly women who help carry my burdens as I help carry theirs. As adults, busy with our own households and lives, building friendship takes more intention than it did in high school and college, where we were thrown in with others and found our place. Often, we must seek out friendships, and we definitely have to work at them.

When my daughter was little, she took ballet. I saw an acquaintance there, another mom I had met when our daughters were in preschool together, someone I had wanted to get to know better. We spent one hour every week for an entire school year talking and sharing while our girls were in class. We built a deep friendship over those months and eventually joined a Bible study together.

Today, she is one of my confidants, and we text each other whenever we have prayer requests. We built a friendship that is an encouragement and support to both of us.

Take a Break When You Need One

This is much easier after we find our people. We are working hard 24 hours a day—earning a living, running a household, and raising kids on our own. "Downtime" becomes more important than ever and equally hard to come by. We need to choose rest and refreshment when we can, even if it's in tiny bite-sized moments.

Maybe someone can watch your kids for an hour so you can go to Target alone. (I know, living the dream!) Go to a park where you can see the kids on the playground while you and your friend walk on the path or sit on a bench and chat.

One of my girls got invited on her first sleep over, and since I knew and trusted the family, I jumped at the chance. I had never allowed sleep overs before, but we were really struggling that week, and we both needed a break. She had a wonderful extended time with her friend, and I cleaned the house and got a bit of rest.

Find Your Children's Triggers

Watch your children and learn what triggers their fear and sadness. Maybe there is a certain posture you use that triggers fear in them because of past trauma. Stop doing it. I am totally serious.

One of my kiddos was getting crazy while I was trying to get her to sleep, and I walked over to her bed, leaned down quickly, and made a silly face, trying to be funny. I didn't run at her. I didn't yell. I was being goofy.

But something about that movement triggered her, and she panicked. I told her she looked terrified, and she replied, "I am."

Ouch.

It hurts when we trigger our kids' fears, no matter how unintentionally it happens.

Please hear this: let that guilt go. If you could not have guessed that your actions would trigger any kind of fear, it is not your fault. Now that you see the trigger, even if you never know what is behind it, you can avoid it.

Do your best to learn your kids' triggers and avoid them. And forgive yourself when you don't.

Make Other Plans

Father's Day is a land mine for my family. My dad died many years ago, and my daughters are both without their dads in their everyday lives.

If you're in the same situation, maybe you'll need to do something different on the day of Father/Daughter dances and Parents' Day at school. My girls get sad when there are father/daughter events at school and church, so we find something else to do. Maybe that's a good time for a family movie night at home or a trip to the cheap theater.

Do something fun to replace the event that causes sadness.

I believe men should be honored on Father's Day. I think it's great when the pastor stands up front and tells the dads how important they are and how needed they are in their kids' lives. He reminds them of their roles and challenges them to lead their families well.

But for us, those ten minutes are agonizing. We know how important dads are, and we don't have one in our home. So, we don't go to that service anymore. We attend our small group studies and youth group, and then we head out before the main sermon. I love my church, and I talk to my kids about why we aren't staying for the service.

We love God and He is the center of our home. I know He understands our pain. He hurts when His children hurt, and I truly believe He doesn't mind that we skip the main church service on Father's Day. The days of sadness and triggered pain that would follow are too much, especially when they are avoidable.

Say No

Don't take on more than you have to outside your home.

Beth, who had been a single mom for years, spoke to our single moms' group at church. I will never forget what she said. During her single mom years, she turned down every volunteer activity at her kids' schools. No brownie baking, no fundraiser organizing, no helping out in the classroom.

And no guilt.

She simply wasn't at a point in life where she had time to do those things.

If there are volunteer activities that you love and that bring you joy, by all means, keep doing them. If you are feeling stressed out by adding one more commitment to the calendar, just say no. You are doing the hard and beautiful work of raising precious hearts and guiding young minds. That might be enough to keep you busy.

Get Professional Help

Many of us, and our children, struggle with PTSD, depression, anxiety, and more, depending on what we have lived through. It is essential that we are aware of our children's behaviors and get them help when needed.

According to the Mayo Clinic, signs of PTSD include irritability, hypervigilance (always being on guard), severe anxiety, loss of interest in activities, nightmares, and more[1]. Symptoms of depression include sadness, hopelessness, anger, tiredness, trouble concentrating, loss of interest in activities, and more[2].

Common symptoms of anxiety include difficulty handing uncertainty, indecisiveness, perceiving threats where there are none, trouble concentrating, and trouble sleeping[3]. When we see these symptoms in ourselves or our children, we need to get help. A regular doctor is a great place to start, as they can offer direct help and referrals to counselors when appropriate.

Even though this process won't be easy, now is the time to take steps toward healing for you and your children. My hope for you is that you will get the help you need now, not ten years from now. There are places that provide counseling for free or at reduced rates. There are online counselors you can have virtual visits or chats with, so you don't even need to find a babysitter. Just a small block of time while the kids are in school or sleeping. Counseling is not out of reach for you.

It is incredibly brave to get the help you and your children need to overcome your hurdles. Talk to your doctor, your church, or trusted friends. They can help direct you to the professionals who can walk with you as you heal.

> Our God is
> Jehovah-Rahpa,
> the God
> who heals.

And remember, our God is Jehovah-Rapha, the God who heals. Not only physical hurts, but emotional and spiritual ones as well. "You have turned my wailing into dancing" (Psalm 30:11). He takes great joy in bringing you healing and watching you thrive.

Connections

Is there one particular area you and your children struggle in? Do you see any signs of PTSD, depression, or anxiety in yourself or your children?

First Step Forward

List three of these suggestions you want to act on.
(Or come up with your own)

1.

2.

3.

CHAPTER 13

Finding Rest

Between raising kids, working, and keeping a home, rest seems almost impossible. How many times have we heard people say to take care of yourself first or you won't be able to take care of others? It's so hard for any mom, let alone a single mom, to do.

I know you're probably exhausted more often than you would like to be. We all feel the "single mom weariness." Whether it's from working several jobs, working while going to school, caring for everything and everyone without help, or trying to heal young hearts that have been wounded by others, we are spent.

Some days it feels like it's all too much and we can't possibly keep going. When you find yourself in that place, seek out rest. We truly can't carry on doing everything for everyone. And it is all too easy to try so hard to fill in the gaps that we find we are no longer doing anything well. I found myself in this place (again) a few weeks ago.

I had forgotten that I didn't have to do everything. My list had grown so long that I no longer knew what was on it. Projects for work started to fall through the cracks. Laundry piled high. Both kids needed math help for hours a night. I needed to study and learn more about running a business, so I could provide better for my family. I felt the stress building. I felt the tremors of panic a few times a day and staunchly pushed through them.

Until the day I didn't. The day I got one more email about something I had finished at the last minute that wasn't finished after all. And I started crying. I knew I was in over my head, but I didn't know any other way to do it. So that night, after my girls went to sleep, I got out my computer and tried to work. There were so many possible projects to work on, and I didn't know where to start.

I stopped and prayed. I asked God which item I should start with.

His response? REST.

Excuse me? Didn't He hear my list? Didn't He know I had bills to pay and projects to do? Didn't He see the pile of laundry? He did. He saw it all. And He wanted me to rest anyway.

I wonder if He is saying the same thing to many of us, but we are too busy to stop and listen. I searched up one of the most well-known verses on rest, Matthew 18:25. "Come to me, all you who are weary and burdened, and I will give you rest."

Many of us know it well. Maybe too well. Well enough that we don't pay attention to it and truly lean into its meaning.

"Come to me."

This isn't a pointed command. It's a gentle, soothing offer. Like words I might speak to one of my girls having a really hard day when I call her over to the sofa to lean against me. A soft, loving voice, calling out a reminder that you are not alone.

"All you who are weary and burdened."

All. Everyone. Every single person is included in this offer. Not only those who have a great income. Not only those who don't have as many responsibilities as others, so they have more time to rest. All. Even those (and maybe, especially those) who don't feel they can rest. Those who feel rest is wasteful because there are so many things to do. Those who worry it will all fall apart if they take time to rest. Even you.

This is the rest we need: resting in God's loving care, letting Him carry us for awhile.

"I will give you rest."

This is good rest. Complete rest. This is rest that will refresh and heal and restore. This is the rest we need: resting in God's loving care, letting Him carry us for a while. God's rest is so much better than the rest the world offers. It is healing restorative rest. And we can enjoy it while letting Him take care of everything else.

Intentional Rest

When I looked up "rest" in the Bible, I was shocked at how many verses came up. In the Old and New Testament alike, the Lord tells us over and over again to come to Him for rest.

"The Lord replied, 'My Presence will go with you, and I will give you rest'" (Exodus 33:14).

"Yes, my soul, find rest in God; my hope comes from him" (Psalm 62:5).

"Whoever dwells in the shelter of the Most High will rest in the shadow of the Almighty" (Psalm 91:1).

"Take my yoke upon you and learn from me, for I am gentle and humble in heart, and you will find rest for your souls" (Matthew 11:29).

"Then, because so many people were coming and going that they did not even have a chance to eat, he said to them, 'Come with me by yourselves to a quiet place and get some rest'" (Mark 6:31).

So many people wanted their attention that the disciples didn't have a chance to eat. It sounds like my house and probably like yours. Sounds like those days that get away from us, and before we realize it, it's 2:30 in the afternoon, and we forgot to eat lunch. And maybe breakfast. Or the days our kids get out the door for school, and we're eating their breakfast leftovers. Sound familiar?

God is serious about offering us rest. He didn't say, "Work until you can't stand up anymore, then do your best to keep going." He created us. He knows us all the way through. He knows how desperately we need rest and refreshment on a regular basis. If we are feeling like it's all about to come crashing down, we need to find a way to rest.

So here are some ideas to help us find rest and refreshment. Let's look for ways to sneak in short moments of rest when we can and to get larger periods of rest when we need them. Or better yet, before we need them.

Keep a special treat in the cupboard

For me, that's low-calorie Sprechers Root Beer. It's expensive, so I don't buy it often, and I don't usually share it with my girls. (They don't care what brand of root beer they drink.) I save my favorite for me.

On a really challenging day, I feel a bit better knowing a root beer is waiting for me to enjoy after my girls go to bed. (Maybe your treat is crackers or chocolate or chips! Whatever you like best!)

Get moving

I know, a lot of people say this. Some things are clichés because they are true! Our bodies need to move. Movement is good for our minds, our bodies and our souls. We may not have an hour to spend at a gym, but in the middle of a long day, we can take a few minutes to march a bit by our desks, or better yet, if no one is around, we can crank up the music and dance.

When someone offers to care for your child or have them over for a play date, accept!

I love my girls. Seriously over-the-top love them. And sometimes, I need some time to myself to rest or get things done. I know this chapter is about resting but having two hours to myself to do laundry and clean up the house can feel so good. I feel better about life in general when our house isn't in complete disarray.

Give your children jobs to do around the house

Many of us struggle with single mom guilt, so we don't ask our kids to help at home. That won't serve them well in the long run, when they are grown and on their own, needing to do things for themselves. Not long ago, I gave my girls each a couple of jobs that they are solely responsible for. One takes out the garbage and picks up after the dog. One empties the dishwasher and takes out the recycling.

It used to be a struggle to get them to help when I would ask them to do something each time it needed to be done. Now that I have assigned the tasks permanently, suddenly, the arguing and procrastination stopped. I mention the job, and they do it. Rarely, if they are overwhelmed with homework or having a really hard day, I'll give them grace and do their job for them. They are truly grateful when that happens and happy to do it themselves the next time.

Spend time with friends

Last night my girls needed a break from schoolwork, so I texted a friend, and we went to her home so my girls could swim in her pool. It had been an overwhelming day, so I decided the best thing I could possibly do was get some fun for my girls and a small break for me. I walked into my friend's house, and the look on her face said it all. Her day had been every bit as awful as ours.

We hugged and laughed and cried together while the kids swam. And suddenly I knew everything would be OK. Sometimes we just need the company of a good friend for a short time to remind us we are not alone.

Another friend has started coming over one night a week. After years of being mostly on our own, hunkered down trying to push through, this is an incredible shift. She doesn't care what my house looks like. And when she comes over, neither do I. We work together to make dinner, our kids play, and we talk. Life lived together is so much better.

Take an hour off and do your favorite thing

Read a book. Take a bath. Take a walk. Something, anything, that refreshes you. I used to work every night after my girls went to sleep. I am slowly learning to take a night off now and then and rest. I sit on the couch with my dog on my lap and watch old episodes of a TV show I know by heart. It still makes me laugh, and I still love the characters. A little bit of laughter does me a whole lot of good.

Pray and read your Bible

Often the very best action we can take is going to God with our weariness. We can tell Him anything and everything. Every detail that is on our minds, keeping us up at night, all the items on our to-do list. Everything. He knows it all already, and He wants a relationship with us. That's how relationships grow: by sharing our hearts with one another. Our relationship with God is the same.

We grow closer to Him when we spend time with Him and share our needs. I often go to favorite Scripture passages after praying when I am struggling. Great wisdom and peace can be found in the Bible and may bring the rest and refreshment you need.

Whenever and however you can, whether it's a ten-minute break from work, an hour after the kids go to sleep, or a weekend while they're on a church retreat, please make a way to get some rest. I promise the world will not fall apart if you do!

Connections

What task can you give up or do less often to find
a few minutes to rest? What is a favorite treat you
can keep on hand that makes you feel good? What
household tasks can you assign to your kids?

First Step Forward

List three things you will do to find a
few minutes of rest this week.

1.

2.

3.

CHAPTER 14

Single Mom Joy

You read that right. JOY. Joy overflowing.

I deeply understand moments of heartache as a single mom, but I want you to know that the moments of joy outnumber them. There is something about having walked through the hard together that makes my relationship with my oldest daughter unique.

We had only each other for such a long time. For many years, I was the one who got to tuck her in every night. I held her when she was sick or sad. I read so many books to her. I played ponies until I thought I would lose my mind. And she and I grew so close.

Frankie knew she could always depend on me. Whatever happened in the world around us didn't matter much, as long as we were together.

When my ex-husband left, my little treasure of a girl was so young that she had no idea what had happened. Her pure innocence and joy radiated from her and lit a spark in me. I tried to keep things as normal as possible for her.

We went to the library. We built tiny snowmen as quickly as we could before the snow melted. I pushed her in the stroller for a mile to get Chinese takeout and fresh air. When we weren't visiting family, it was just the two of us, and we had fun. We played and laughed and sang silly songs.

Facebook keeps populating memories from the months after my ex-husband left—the time that was so dark in my life. Yet the memories that pop up are of pure joy.

My little girl in her snowsuit surrounded by no more than an inch of snow, with grass still poking up, leaning down by her carefully built, 10-inch-tall snowman.

Next to our little Christmas tree, her eyes sparkling with joy and wonder at having hung up an ornament all by herself.

A sweet close-up with her curls perfectly framing her dimpled face.

While I remember the context of these photos and the grief I was in, I also distinctly remember the unabashed joy of those moments and the light that pierced the darkness with each one. It was as if my whole world was in the deepest, darkest, moonless night, and one by one, the stars began to shine.

We loved going to the library and finding new books. Our favorite was Two to Cuddle by Eileen Spinelli, an incredibly sweet book celebrating the love of a mom and a child. I must have read it to her a hundred times until she could say the words right along with me.

We memorized it, and she pored over the pictures. We held tightly to each other. The security I couldn't give her earlier in life, I gave her in spades now. She would always know she was loved. She would always know she was cherished. She would always know joy and laughter. She would always be safe.

There are plenty of things that are challenging about being a single mom. My relationship with my daughter isn't one of them. Sure, there are days that are hard. There are times we disagree. But we know beyond any doubt that we are a team, that we are always there for each other.

Frankie knows that I am her biggest cheerleader and will always be on her side. Life with her is so much fun. We have a bond like I have never imagined a parent could have with a child. We are freakishly close and love each other's company.

She's a teenager now, so I know our relationship is changing, and I trust we will always be close. I'm praying we will skip over the teenage attitude and go right to an adult friendship. (Let me dream, people. Let me dream.)

Create your Fun

Take a few moments to consider your daily life. Do you make time for joy? Have you started new traditions (or continued old ones)? We must be purposeful in building our new lives.

> It was as if my whole world was in the deepest, darkest, moonless night, and one by one, the stars began to shine.

The life we thought we would have is gone forever, and we need to be intentional in building our bright new future. Start with a small step or two. Find a book you all love. Find a favorite food or movie. Or both! When you are having a hard week, when tempers flare, have something in common you can pull out quickly to change the mood.

For example, my girls and I talk in funny accents all the time. All. The. Time.

I wonder what other people would think if they could get a peek into our home when no one else is around. We are purposeful about creating silliness. And since I'm the mom, I get to lead the way. I do accents, make faces, do a goofy walk. Whatever I can to break up the day and make it more fun.

We love to play Uno and will randomly grab the cards for a quick game between homework and dinner. We try putting a bit of fun into otherwise dreary activities. We play loud music while we clean, have contests to see how much we can accomplish in 30 minutes. I set the timer on the microwave, and we start hustling. The faster we clean, the more time we have for fun.

What can you do today to seek out and build joy for your family? Find a few moments to set aside the work and the struggle. Ignore the dishes. Let the laundry stay in the basket. Be silly with your children. Dance in the kitchen and sing in the rain. Talk in silly accents while you make dinner.

I promise you there is so much joy and laughter to be found in being a single mom. Each time you create a moment of joy, your children notice. They start playing along. It delights my daughters when I am silly and weird. Last night, two of us were in the car together and were simply talking nonsense. I said something completely bizarre, and my daughter roared with laughter.

I can't for the life of me remember what I said, but I will never forget her eyes sparkling and her laughter filling the car. Those are the moments I want to create and treasure. Those are the moments we need more of.

"But let all who take refuge in you be glad; let them ever sing for joy. Spread your protection over them, that those who love your name may rejoice in you"(Psalm 5:11).

Connections
What activities, big or small, bring you joy?
What brings your kids joy?

First Step Forward
Write down three things you can do to
bring joy to your days this week.

1.

2.

3.

NOT OVER YET

CHAPTER 15

Forgiving Yourself

Many single moms find it hard to forgive the ones who hurt them or their children and harder still to forgive themselves, even for situations that weren't their fault and may have been out of their control. They carry that guilt, the shame following them like a shadow they can't escape.

Natalie's Story

My friend, Natalie, has been a single mom for twelve years. Natalie says, "The hardest memory for me is when I saw my husband hurt my child. That day haunts me, stalks me, won't let me go. My little girl was terrified, and I stood frozen. Unable to move. Astounded and shocked. I will never forget that day and can't seem to forgive myself for not protecting her. I am not guilty of abusing my child, but I live with the guilt of not protecting her. I wish I could go back to that day and tell him to put her down and get out. I can't believe I was still trying to save my marriage, despite his actions."

So many single moms live with this intense guilt of abuse they saw, of living in conditions that were harmful to their kids, or of not being able to protect their children. Guilt that isn't theirs to carry. And yet, it weighs heavily on their hearts every day.

Carrying that guilt is not our job. Truly, it's another burden added into the baggage we lug around every day. Like a huge boulder, adding weight without value. We need to find a way to lay that guilt down and walk away.

Natalie carried her guilt boulder for years. Not for something she did, but something she didn't do. She says Satan likes to remind her of it so she will stay locked in the past, unable to build a great future for herself and her children. He will throw it back at her at the oddest moments. When she is completely wrapped up in something else, those few awful minutes come back into her thoughts.

Maybe it's the same for you. Some memory, maybe many memories all flowing together, bringing enormous life-changing guilt. That's where Satan wants us: trapped by the past, by bad memories, and by guilt, even if that guilt was never ours to begin with.

We have to fight back. We have to stand up and fight for our own hearts. We fight with truth, remembering what actually happened and who is truly responsible, and refusing to carry any guilt that doesn't belong to us. We fight by reminding ourselves that we can't change the past and that we are only human.

We can choose to learn from those circumstances and make sure they are never repeated. Taking care of ourselves and our children now is what matters.

Annie's Story

Annie, another friend who is a single mom, says, "I do blame myself for poor choices I have made in my life, especially raising my children. I should have left the abusive situation earlier. I should have chosen a better father for them. I sometimes have put my needs or wants above theirs. I don't know if I will ever truly forgive myself, but I choose to try and look forward. Remember where I have been and learn from it. Try not to repeat the same mistakes and accept what I can and cannot do about the situation now. I lament to Jesus, and He hears my pain and sorrows and comforts me when I need Him to."

Annie knows the only thing that can help is taking it all to Jesus—every bit of our guilt and pain and regret. All of it. We need to remember to take it to Him each and every time we feel it and let His love and forgiveness wash over us. Let Him heal our hearts and move mountains to remind us how much He loves us.

Once we give our lives to God and ask for His forgiveness, all of our sins are washed away. He certainly doesn't hold us accountable for the actions of others. God doesn't want us living in regret and shame. He came to set us free from all of that. Every last bit. "It is for freedom that Christ has set us free" (Galatians 5:1).

> Walk away from the chains and into the freedom that the grace of God offers us so abunandtly.

Jesus is the ultimate chain-breaker. And still, we grab the chains He died to break, wrap them around ourselves, and pull them tight. We try so hard to hold on to our chains and keep them wrapped around us.

It is time to let go.

Let those chains fall to the ground, powerless, never to hold you again. Walk away from the chains into the freedom that the grace of God offers us so abundantly. You were designed for freedom in Christ.

Satan will go on reminding us of our chains. He knows how well they held us before. He will keep trying to hand them to us. I'm not telling you this to scare you, but you can only be prepared to fight if you know what is coming. Every time the guilt and shame start creeping in again, we need to lay them at Jesus' feet.

We need to remind ourselves that God is doing a new work in us. The past can't hold us anymore because Jesus says so. Satan can try as hard as he wants to get those chains back around us. In God's power and by God's abundant grace, we have the right to refuse to wear the chains ever again.

Let today be the day that you turn from the guilt and find that God's mercy and grace are enough for you.

Connections
Is there an event or circumstance that you struggle to forgive yourself for? Is there something out of your control that you still feel guilty about?

First Step Forward
If you are struggling with forgiving yourself, ask God to help you. He wants you to live in the freedom He provides.

CHAPTER 16

The Other Parent

I have heard of divorced parents who work seamlessly together as they co-parent with the children's best interest in mind, making decisions and discussing problems together. For most of the single moms I know, this is definitely not the case.

Many struggle with visits and child support payments and are truly making most of the decisions about their children's lives on their own. Even for the single moms who have their children with them most of the time, there are usually issues to deal with regarding the other parent.

Visits

I wonder if visits will ever get easy. I handle it much better than I did when visits first started, and I would dive into deep sadness when I dropped her off. I've gotten used to the house being quieter and having only one kid here.

Still, I miss her laughter and her sweetness. I miss hearing her call to me from upstairs, and I miss her goofiness. Some days, dropping her off still feels like giving a part of my heart away. Her dad and I meet halfway in a Kohl's parking lot, and I see other families at the same spot for the same reason. Sadness always pours over me when I think about how many kids are exchanging one home for another for the weekend. It must be a hard way to live and nothing I ever wanted for my precious girl.

However, our kids want a relationship with both of their parents, no matter what has happened in the past. It's built into every person to want to know their parents, to be able to depend on them, to know we are loved by them. If the other parent is willing, interested, and a safe person for the kids to be with, visits can be a great experience. Even if visits are less than ideal, your child may want or be required to go.

Do your best to work with the other parent to help visits happen, as long as it doesn't compromise your child's safety. If you learn that your child is in danger in the other home, please get help. I have seen too many moms let it go for fear or the financial stress another court case would bring. I've heard the stories, and I also know that our kids need to feel and be safe. Nothing is more important than protecting the ones entrusted to us.

Transition time, as the child leaves or comes home, can be hard on the child. It's such a stark reminder that their life is not how they want it to be. A reminder of what could have been and will never be.

During times of transition, I find it imperative not to plan big events or have extra people in our home. And I am almost never gone during a transition. My daughter always wants me to drop her off and pick her up, feels safer coming home to me, and has an easier time settling back in when I am present.

Find what works best for your kids and do all you can to make that happen as often as possible. Don't worry about what others think; do what's right for your family.

Discipline

Having two sets of boundaries and consequences can be hard for your children. If you and the other parent are able to, work together to set expectations and follow similar house rules. That is often not tenable.

I have rules in our house that give my girls important boundaries and lessons. Even if they are different than what my oldest daughter has elsewhere, I still expect her to follow the rules at home. I explain the rules and the reasons behind them so she knows they are not arbitrary. The rules are in place to keep my kids safe and train them to be great adults. The more I share the reasoning behind the rules, the more willing my girls are to follow them.

According to todaysparent.com[4], single moms who have come out of abusive relationships may need to choose parallel parenting instead of co-parenting for their mental health and safety. By parallel parenting rather than co-parenting, survivors make everyday decisions about the kids and consult with their exes only when larger decisions, such as choosing schools, need to be made together. If you have sole custody or an absent ex, make sure you have a great support system for when you want help making big decisions.

Along with creating the right relationship with an ex, we also need to be thinking about how to talk about them to our children. Our kids know they are half us and half their fathers. If we talk badly about their dads, it can translate in their minds to talking badly about them. We must work hard to understand the world through our children's minds, to consider how they will hear and experience our words.

Telling the Truth

My girls both have questions about why they aren't with their dads. I do everything in my power to never talk badly about their dads. They love their dads, and talking badly about them would only hurt my children. However, I am not covering for them either. There are honest-to-goodness bad choices that have been made that affected my daughters' entire lives. When they are old enough, and they ask me, I will tell them the unbiased truth, coated in absolute love.

The more time that passes, the more I am able to look at some of the experiences of their lives with less and less emotion. One of my girls feels very responsible for something that happened in her life that she literally couldn't have had one ounce of control over. Yet, she blamed herself for years. That I will not allow. I can't let her go on believing this horrible thing that happened to her was her fault. I cannot and will not let her live in the guilt and shame of something someone else did.

One day, when she was filled with regret and struggling with that memory, I asked her when she did it. When she made that life-altering decision.

She couldn't tell me because it wasn't her decision.

No part of it could have been influenced by her. I asked her who actually made the decision and she told me. I made sure she knew the decision was never hers to make, that the regret and guilt were never hers to carry. That it was time to lay them down and move forward.

I cannot prevent the truthful conclusions she will come to as she gets older and can see the situation through different eyes. But I can make sure she knows enough truth about it now to be freed from that guilt.

My Memories

I am not yet fully healed from everything that happened in my marriage. I'm still pursuing healing, and these days are immeasurably brighter than those first months after my marriage ended. I want my oldest daughter to know that we had good times in our family. That I loved her dad very much and planned to spend my whole life with him.

I make a point to tell her happy stories from our life together. As she begins asking about what happened and why we aren't married anymore, I want her to have a balanced view, to see the lovely and the hard, to see the truth, and to know that she was loved through it all.

Talk it out

I always encourage my girls to talk to me about whatever might be on their minds. Stuffing the difficult, painful topics down and never dealing with them will hurt them so much in the long run. Pain that is stuffed down inside just turns into anger, deeper pain, and sickness later.

My girls probably get pretty tired of hearing me ask them to talk about their thoughts and feelings. My goal is to deal with whatever hard things they are facing now, rather than have those things become bigger problems down the line. Even when they don't want to talk, they know I am here no matter what. No judgment, just waiting in love to handle their deepest fears and pain.

Navigating the Challenges

The issues regarding the other parent seem to be the hardest part of the journey for me. Walking the fine line of respecting the other parent while acknowledging past mistakes is such a delicate balance. Removing emotion from conversations about the past is challenging for those of us who wear our hearts on our sleeves. Enforcing rules that only apply in my home and helping my girls navigate this confusing part of life is not something we are taught in school.

None of it makes much sense if I dig too deep.

That's part of living in this world full of bad choices, hurtful actions, and painful circumstances. It's not supposed to make sense because this is not how God designed the world in the beginning. We are supposed to do the best we can in God's power to live for Him while navigating these rough waters.

> Give yourself grace when you do it wrong and remind yourself you get to try again.

Give yourself grace when you do it wrong and remind yourself that you get to try again.

It's critical to not try to do this on your own. Seek wisdom from others who have gone before you or from trusted friends who know your situation intimately. Ask God for guidance and ask Him to give you the words to say. Recently, I didn't know how to move forward in dealing with a particular item about our past. I had been praying for weeks, seeking wisdom about how to proceed. Then I ran into one of my dear friends at a store and shared my concerns with her. She knew exactly who to go to for help and connected us within the hour. Find the people who love you and your children well and follow it up with action. They will be invaluable helpers on this journey.

Connections

In what areas of parenting are you different from your children's father? What do your kids need in order to feel stable and secure in your home?

First Step Forward

Write down three good memories of your marriage or early family life you can share with your children.

1.

2.

3.

NOT OVER YET

CHAPTER 17

Surviving Abuse

I don't think I will ever understand why the abused person feels the shame, but I know it to be true. I have seen it in the eyes and heard it in the voices of so many women who lived with neglect or abuse for many years, afraid or not wanting to leave, not wanting anyone to know how they were living.

After all, some would have us believe that if abuse happens in a Christian marriage, the woman must not have done her part and maybe even deserved what was being done to her. Maybe she was told she needed to be a better wife so the abuse would stop. Maybe that shame is hiding in your eyes and voice as well.

I am here to tell you to set it down. It was not your fault. No matter what type of abuse you lived with, no matter what horrors you have survived, you deserve a future free of shame and guilt. You absolutely, unequivocally, and without question did not deserve what you have been through. No one ever has the right to abuse another person. Not for any reason. It is not your fault.

Annie's Story

Remember my friend Annie, who has trouble forgiving herself for not making better choices for her children? She bravely shares more of her story.

I always wanted to be a mom. I grew up without my dad and vowed that my children would never go through that. They would have their dad in their lives, and we would be a happy family. When I met John, he was charming and treated me well. I thought I had found true love. We fought a lot, but I thought that was a normal part of a relationship.

During one argument, about eight months into our relationship, John put my hand through a window and slammed me into a wall. The next day I found out I was pregnant. I asked my sister for advice and was told that sometimes arguments get violent, and I should try to work it out. He begged for forgiveness, and we went into counseling. I wanted to save our relationship more than anything. I didn't want my baby to grow up without his dad.

During my pregnancy, the violence became worse and much more frequent. When I was eight months pregnant, John threw me down the stairs. I was so scared that something had happened to my baby. I knew my baby was being abused right along with me. The emotional abuse led me to believe this was what I deserved. Once the baby was born, I thought I wouldn't be hurt if I was holding him. I was so wrong. John threw my son out of my arms and threw me to the ground. I left and moved to another county to try to start over without him. He followed me.

Again, he begged for forgiveness and said he would go to anger management classes. What I didn't know then is that this cycle was something that had been repeated with countless other women.

As long as I was really good, it was good. I learned all these rules of things I could do and things I couldn't do, and I tried really hard to stay within those parameters. If I managed to be good enough and not break any of his rules, I thought I would be safe.

The emotional, physical, and mental abuse were intense. The shame brought on by the abuse was overwhelming. Absolutely no one knew what we were living in. The good days were so very good. We looked like a normal happy family on the outside.

Behind closed doors, we were in agony. The outside appearance was so beautiful, and I wanted the inside to match.

When my son was two or three, John started taking his anger out on him. I tried to keep my son away from him. I was hiding my son's behavior so he wouldn't get beaten. When he was in kindergarten or first grade I told his dad, "If you want to hit him, you hit me." My son and I became a team to try and keep his dad off us. A secret society to not anger Dad.

Eventually, it wasn't enough to hit me; he wanted to defeat me. The abuse became almost unbearable, but I didn't know how to get out. The abuse happened behind closed doors and in front of the children. I was unable to keep my private world private anymore, and it was exploding. He came to my job and threatened my supervisor. He came to a family gathering and threatened to kill me. I was terrified.

I remember my son telling me one day, why can't daddy just go away? And I realized I wasn't doing anybody any favors by keeping him around.

I didn't know anyone who had been in this situation. It's not something you Google. I didn't know how to get out. It took me ten years to get out. I finally got a restraining order and spent the next four years trying to put my life back together emotionally.

I can't make it all go away. That's their dad. I can't restrict them from seeing him because I wasn't able to prove anything he did to me. Even when I ended up in the emergency room and almost died, it wasn't enough. No one had seen it happen. Without witnesses, it was his word against mine.

My restraining order ended, and I was unable to renew it. I had to set different kinds of boundaries after that, and they're not court-ordered. The boundaries are so important to set up for physical and emotional safety. I also prepare my children to deal with their dad. To understand the idea that they don't get to pick their parents, that's their dad. He's not perfect. He's flawed severely. I gave my children a good emotional structure to be able to go through that. Visitations with their dad are hard. He was arrested last night on the way to the visitation. We're still going through it. My kids are fourteen and eight and are still having a very roller coaster relationship with their dad.

I wish he could have fixed himself to enjoy us and the kids. But I know we're better off this way. I'm glad that it's over. I hadn't realized what a weight it was to carry every day. I am working on getting all of that weight and shame gone. And I am realizing that it's not my fault.

Escaping abuse is not like it is in the movies. You don't just call the cops, and he's gone, and you're safe. The leaving is where the battle truly begins, and you need a lot of support to get through the rest.

Leaving can take many attempts. Keep trying. Reach out to someone you know you can trust who will support you. You only have to tell one person you trust who will stand by you through it all. My family came alongside me and went to all of my court dates with me. I found a survivor group, found an advocate that helped me file all of the paperwork. You have to tell people that you need help because they don't know otherwise. And that's hard. Because there is so much stigma with being an abused woman. As if, somehow, it's your fault. I tried two or three survivor groups before I found the one that seemed to fit and stuck with it until the end. I couldn't have done it alone. Just keep going. Keep trying.

With him removed from the home, my kids have been able to flourish in an emotionally healthy home. That's something that was lacking before. I love being a mom; I always wanted to be a mom. Family game nights and dinner times were not part of our home life before because it was so stressful and so bad. And now we have each other, and I'm able to emotionally support them in a way I couldn't before.

Being able to sit down and watch a movie together and listen to my son's day and give him little tidbits on how he could handle a situation or breakups with girlfriends or fights with friends is great stuff.

I was so crushed by the weight of the abuse before that I couldn't be present with him. I don't remember my daughter's first three years of life because of the stress of the abuse. I feel bad that I don't remember her learning to walk; I don't remember potty training her. It was really a rough time. I can't get that stuff back, but I can form so many more memories and bonds with her now. And she doesn't remember that stuff either. She'll remember this, the snuggle times on the couch, and all of the things that weren't in our life before.

Hope for the Future

I am so grateful to Annie for sharing her story. If you are in a similar situation to hers, I pray that you find hope in her words. Leaving is incredibly hard. But not impossible. Even if you have tried before and ended up back in the relationship, you get to try again. It's not too late.

Every kind of abuse causes emotional damage. You may not be able to see your worth or understand yet that it's not your fault. You may have a hard time believing that there could be a better future for you. A future without shame and guilt. A future without fear. If you can't see the light yet, if you can't feel even a flicker of hope, please know that I am hoping and praying for you. I see your pain. I understand your shame. And I promise you there is hope.

"'For I know the plans I have for you,' declares the Lord, 'Plans to prosper you and not to harm you, plans to give you hope and a future'" (Jeremiah 29:11).

That's one of God's promises to you. To YOU. He has great plans for hope and a future for you. You can trust him. The One who promised is faithful (Hebrews 10:23).

Connections

Have you made excuses for your partner's behavior, believing that you deserved what was done to you? Are you in danger in your home? Please be honest with yourself and decide if you need protection from abuse.

First Step Forward

If you are in danger, please consider these steps.

1. Find a local women's shelter you could go to.
2. Tell one trustworthy friend what has been happening.
3. Make a plan to get help as soon as possible.

Please see page 215 for a list of resources to help domestic abuse survivors.

CHAPTER 18

Your Backstory
& Parenting

My family's backstory is not easy.

Most people in my life don't know the things I have lived through. They don't need to. There are parts of our story and parts of yours that don't need to be told to more than your closest confidants.

Some of those pieces of the story have changed who you are. They have changed how you relate to your kids and to others. Maybe you have built a wall to keep yourself safe. Maybe separation from your kids is hard because they were hurt by someone in the past. Maybe you struggle to trust any man because of what one man did to you.

You are not alone.

Annie and Natalie (from the chapter "Forgiving Yourself") are my friends. I have seen their pain when their kids have had to visit their dads. It's not that they are over-protective, helicopter moms who can't let go. They have witnessed abuse. They have experienced it themselves and have seen their children suffer.

Of course they are going to have a hard time sending their children to the abusers. The world doesn't see it. The world doesn't know. To others, it looks like they are over-reacting. But the truth is, they are living a nightmare other people simply aren't aware of.

Their One Safe Place

One of my trips to Uganda to meet my younger daughter, and go through the Ugandan process of legal guardianship, stretched from two weeks into a long three-and-a-half. When I arrived in Uganda, it took several days for me to get a phone, and the video chat program on my computer wasn't working.

I'd left Frankie home with my mom, thinking it was best for her, but I didn't get to talk to her at home for almost a week. It was torture for both of us. All those years of being each other's one and only constant companion are beautiful. And they make it so hard when we must be apart. I was her one safe place, and she couldn't even talk to me, let alone come find me when she was afraid.

Looking back, I wish I had taken her with me. If I had known how hard it was going to be, I would have taken her in a heartbeat. No question. I don't care how much school she would miss or how hard the long hot days in Uganda would be when we had nothing to do and nowhere to go. I would take her with me.

A lot of people don't understand that.

They don't have any idea why our time apart is hard. During my trip, someone teased me, laughing and saying, "Oh, does she think her mommy's not coming back?" She had no idea how much truth was in there. For many children who have lived through their parents' divorce or abandonment, that is an intense fear they live with daily—wondering if this parent is going to leave, too. And making sure my daughter knows that I will never leave her is one of my most important goals.

Annie told me that people questioned her all the time about letting her kids sleep in her room so long. I heard the same concerns, and we eventually learned not to talk to other people about it. The extra judgment wasn't helpful. We knew what our kids had been through and what they needed. We were warned that our kids would never learn to stand on their own, be independent. I believe the opposite to be true.

Once my daughters and I were all finally home together, my girls wanted to be close to me. I had moved into the smaller bedroom and given them the large master bedroom since they were sharing a room. I loved my new room. It was cozy and a perfect fit for me, without any wasted space. It ended up a lot cozier when both of my daughters moved in! They each had a space on the floor where they slept at night, complete with blankets, pillows, stuffed animals, and eventually, even a mattress.

We lived that way for five months. All of us cozied up, safe, sound, and together in my little room. I had to be very careful not to step on anyone when I got up at night, and I often was awoken by feet and legs bumping into my bed. I was constantly tired, and I didn't care. It was just what they needed. When they felt ready, they went back to their own room, knowing full well that they were welcome back whenever they felt the need (and they haven't returned yet).

Allowing them in my room gave them felt safety anytime and every time they needed it. Being near me allowed my girls to build security and confidence until they felt secure enough to want to be in their own space. Dr. Karyn Purvis, author of The Connected Child, defines "felt safety" as "when you arrange the environment and adjust your behavior so your children can feel in a profound and basic way that they are truly safe in their home with you. Until your child experiences safety for himself or herself, trust can't develop, and healing and learning won't progress[5]."

I know my girls. I know their stories. I understand their need to be close and feel safe. And I absolutely love that God chose me to be their safe place. Were there some nights I wanted to sleep in peace all by myself? Absolutely. Would I do it differently next time? Not a chance.

I know my children. I know that when they are good and ready, they will pull away and stand on their own. And I know that for now, I get to be the one to give them security. I get to be the one they come to in the middle of the night. I get to be the one who loses sleep because of the one accidentally kicking my bed all night and the one snoring because she has a cold. It isn't easy, but it is one of the greatest privileges of my life.

The Mama They Need

Annie told me something similar once. She mentioned that people commented on the way she parented her children. That she was overprotective and treating them like much younger kids. But she knew why. Her kids were seriously affected by the abusive situation they lived in for ten years. They deal with PTSD and Separation Anxiety, very real struggles they face every day. Annie knows she has been judged for co-sleeping, coddling, excusing bad behaviors, not being tough enough.

> Make me the mama they need today.

But she is the one who knows what they have lived through and understands how it has affected them. She knows how important it is for her children to have a voice and some control in their lives. She knows they can never be spanked—not after what they have already lived through. She knows what they need, and she prays about it.

The part I love most, the part that truly inspires me, is that she prays, "Make me the mama they need today." What a beautiful thing to think and pray about every day: To be the mom our kids need, no matter what the world may say.

And through the years, her children have grown and blossomed beautifully. I believe it's because she cared for them in the best way she could, despite what others may have said.

If you are in the place of sending your children away with someone who abused them, neglected them, or is mean to them, you are not alone. What is it your children need from you to feel safe in their situation? What is it that others judge you for, but you know is best for your kids?

Don't worry about the negative voices. Don't worry about the judgment of the world. Remember, they haven't lived your story. They don't know the truth, and they don't know the consequences someone else's actions have had on your life and the lives of your children.

Please don't let their judgment change what you are doing. Do what you know is best for your children. No matter what the world says.

If you're unsure, pray about it. Take it to God and ask Him to give you wisdom. Godly wisdom will guide you through every situation, and He promises to give it. "If any of you lacks wisdom, you should ask God, who gives generously to all without finding fault, and it will be given to you" (James 1:5).

I love this promise. I love that God will never leave us alone as single moms. He will always be with us and will guide us whenever we ask Him to.

Connections

What is something that others judge you for that you know is best for your children? Is there an area of parenting that you are unsure how to handle? Who is someone you can ask for advice that is wise and will help without judging?

First Step Forward

List any areas of parenting you would like advice on. Pray about them or talk to a trusted friend or mentor about them.

1.

2.

3.

CHAPTER 19

Grief & Recovery

Sometimes I will be walking through an ordinary day, and my breath will suddenly go out of me as grief stalks me once again. It may be as brief as a snapshot, a physical sensation from the past, or as complex as a complete scene playing out before my eyes.

Not long ago, I saw a man hit a woman a few feet away from me, and I froze. A scene I had witnessed years ago seemed to be placed over the real scene before me, like an overlay. The trauma of that moment years ago was as fresh as if it had truly just happened again. I couldn't move; my mind went blank. I was unable to help. Again.

It took days for me to recover from that moment. Days of seeing the scene flash before me again. Days of fear and helplessness. Days of praying and crying. That's what PTSD can do to a person. I believe that our minds can heal. There is incredible research saying that we can literally re-wire our brains by speaking God's truth over ourselves. And it will take a lot of intentional work.

These moments grief or PTSD are familiar for me, but not usually to this level of intensity. My child might grab my wrist, or I smell something or see an expression. Any of these things might remind me of something in the past, and the emotions starts to overwhelm me.

My mom told me something her counselor, Dan Green, Ph.D., talked to her about repeatedly after my dad's death. He described these moments as STUGs: Sudden Temporary Upsurge of Grief. While he was speaking specifically about grief after death, STUGs apply perfectly to what we experience as well. We are grieving the loss of a relationship, a marriage, and our hopes and plans for the future. As we encounter these moments of grief, it helps to give them a name. And it really helps to remember that second word. Temporary. This, too, will pass.

These moments come unexpectedly and are completely unwelcome. But they are also temporary.

Many women have witnessed or lived through traumatic incidents, and each one is affected by these moments. It's hard to walk through life knowing these memories might jump out at any moment, and it's hard to shake the grief that can seep in and take hold. Please remember that these moments are short-lived. Brighter moments are ahead, and sometimes all we can do is pray and hold on to get through.

I have some ideas that have helped me in these situations. Try them out or come up with what might help you. Just please, don't give up. These STUGs get further and further apart as time goes on and your healing progresses. Even the simplest prayer can be so effective. "The prayer of a righteous person is powerful and effective." (James 5:16).

Maybe it's a quick, "Lord, help." Maybe it's saying the name of Jesus over and over. There truly is power in His name.

Ask for Help

I had one of these moments while writing this book.

I was writing a particularly difficult part, remembering some of my hardest days. My trauma brain took over, my body began to tremble, and tears began to flow. My breath was coming too quickly, and I couldn't even pray. But I could text!

With shaking hands, I texted two of my dearest friends and asked them to pray for me immediately. I didn't need to give them details. It was so beautiful to know that they would drop everything and pray for me.

They covered me in prayers that I couldn't say myself.

I rested in their prayers until I could form my own feeble prayer.

Do you have those people in your life? If not, start praying that God will send them to you. God wants us to be in relationship with other believers. He knows we are going to need others to walk through this difficult world with, and He has a plan in place. Find your people.

It can take great strength to face your trauma and choose healing. And you are worth it.

Get Counseling

Church, women's shelters, even some counseling centers will offer free or reduced-cost counseling to women in need.

Single mom Lauren went to individual counseling and to a domestic violence survivors' group every week for months after leaving her abusive ex-husband. She says it felt good knowing that she wasn't the only one going through that experience. Connecting with other single moms and knowing God is with her also helped her immensely.

I don't know what you have faced in your life, but I do know that God wants to heal you from it. It can take great strength to face your trauma and choose healing. And you are worth it.

Speak What is True Today

When the STUGs send you back to moments in the past, speak what is true today over yourself. If you remember a time when you were in physical danger, tell yourself that you are safe. The doors are locked; no one is trying to hurt you now.

If you remember being verbally abused, fight those words with the truth about yourself. You are loved, you are chosen, you are treasured by the One who created you. Whatever your STUG is, find words that help you fight it. Write them out and keep them close so you can find them and speak them even when your heart is troubled and you are not thinking clearly.

Dwell on Biblical Truth

Reading biblical truth is a powerful tool in these circumstances. Try reading the following verses slowly and intentionally, out loud.

> "The Lord is a refuge for the oppressed, a stronghold in times of trouble. Those who know your name trust in you, for you, Lord, have never forsaken those who seek you" (Psalm 9:9-10).

> "From the end of the earth I will cry to You, when my heart is overwhelmed; lead me to the rock that is higher than I. For You have been a shelter for

me, a strong tower from the enemy" (Psalm 61:2-3 NKJV).

"You will keep in perfect peace those whose minds are steadfast because they trust in you. Trust in the Lord forever, for the Lord, the Lord himself, is the Rock eternal" (Isaiah 26:3-4).

"Because of the Lord's great love, we are not consumed, for his compassions never fail. They are new every morning; great is your faithfulness. I say to myself, 'The Lord is my portion; therefore, I will wait for Him'" (Lamentations 3:22-24).

Whatever you do, don't give up. Healing can happen. With the help of God and close friends, you can move past what happened and build a great new life.

Connections

What grief are you struggling with?
What memories won't let you go?

First Step Forward

Write three things you will try the
next time you hit a STUG.

1.

2.

3.

Earthquakes of the Soul

Trauma is an earthquake of the soul.

When your whole world is shaken, and you feel (or are) physically and emotionally under attack, adrenaline rushes. Fight, flight, or freeze takes over. Maybe you can't breathe. A trauma episode looks different from person to person, depending on the level of trauma and the coping skills someone has.

In some people, these episodes are rare and less noticeable. It might look like normal stress or fear, and they hide it well. In others, a trauma episode can be as intense as appearing to be comatose, completely unresponsive, unable to hear or see, unable to move.

I have experienced both primary trauma (that happened to me) and secondary trauma (from hearing about or witnessing another person's trauma). Many of you have, too.

Sometimes we feel like the walking wounded, trying to get through the regular activities of life during an earthquake of trauma or its aftershocks. The trauma we are living with is not a new occurrence in our lives, but the PTSD that follows old traumas, like an angry wolf growling threateningly at our heels.

A couple of weeks ago, my daughters and I had a major trauma episode in our home. One of us triggered badly enough that the others ended up triggered as well. After nearly two hours of the episode, we were all physically and emotionally exhausted and on our way to church for our Wednesday night studies.

Because, of course, God knew it would happen and orchestrated it to be on a day we would have godly people around us to help us through. On that day, I forgot most of my coping skills as the trauma seemed to come out of nowhere and caught me completely off-guard. So now I have a cheat sheet. A simple piece of paper hanging where I can see it so that when trauma comes again, I can remember what to do.

Our Trauma

Trauma is not fun to talk about. We desperately want to keep it hidden. No one would look at my daughters and me and think that we were suffering from PTSD. I often judge myself, thinking that my trauma is so much less than other people's trauma. That what I went through isn't nearly as bad.

That is absolutely not the point. An earthquake is an earthquake. It's scary, even if it's a small one. An earthquake of the soul is devastating.

We have the chance to cope and heal and experience these earthquakes less often and to a lesser degree, but only if we admit the struggle. If you had a bad sprain and your friend had a broken leg, you would both need time to heal—different injuries, but both painful and in need of extra care.

It's the same with trauma. Don't allow yourself to go down the road of comparing your trauma to someone else's. To think you have it better or worse. Many of us live with some amount of trauma, and we all deserve healing.

I can't wait for Heaven, where we will be fully healed from all of it, but I'm not giving up on healing here on earth either. Whatever trauma you are dealing with, remember it's not the end. We get better. We can heal, and we can learn to cope.

Coping with Trauma

Most children of single moms have lived through some amount of trauma. Whether it's from abuse and neglect or simply having a parent leave the family, our children are affected by what they have gone through.

The results of that are something we need to teach them to cope with and help them heal from. We need to learn the signs of our children's trauma, so we can help them before the episode gets out of control. If we catch a trauma episode early on, we have a much better chance of counteracting it and preventing it from intensifying.

Karyn Purvis was a leading expert on childhood trauma and co-founder of the Karyn Purvis Institute of Child Development at Texas Christian University in Fort Worth, Texas. She coined the term "children from hard places" to describe the children she loved and served, those who have suffered trauma, abuse, neglect, or other adverse conditions early in life[6]. Her research-based philosophy for healing harmed children centered on earning trust and building deep emotional connections to anchor and empower them.

If you are a parent whose child has suffered abuse it is essential to recognize that your child has been through trauma and to learn how to help them cope.

I learned about trauma and its effects on children during the required pre-adoption training I went through before adopting Gloria. There is so much to learn, but we don't need to know it all.

We need to know three key ideas: what causes trauma, what trauma looks like in our children, and what techniques can help them through their trauma. My trauma and theirs often rear up unexpectedly, so we needed to find ways to cope in those moments. Here are some ideas I hope you find helpful in dealing with trauma in your own home.

Pray

If I am thinking clearly, this is the first step in confronting our trauma. Ask God for wisdom and help to get through this. Ask for healing of the wounds and understanding to see what's really happening.

I may do this silently or pray with my child. If she is in a full-blown trauma episode, I pray out loud over her. I want her to know where to run when she needs help, and there is no safer place than God's arms. As I beg God to comfort her and carry her and heal her heart, she is learning to ask Him for the same things. I want to teach her how to ask for help in the hardest moments.

Watch for Triggers

If you pay careful attention, over time, you will learn some of the situations that trigger your children, even if you don't know why they are triggers. Avoid them when you can and teach coping skills for when you can't.

An adoptive mom talks about a day at her daughter's school when people were asked to wear blue if they had lost a loved one.

The goals were to build empathy and for the kids who had suffered a loss to know they weren't alone. It was a horrible week for this mom and her daughter. The daughter felt constantly confronted by her trauma, knowing the blue day was coming. The mom talked it through with her daughter and shared some options. Her daughter decided to go, but not wear blue. She didn't want to be asked about the person she lost. Instead, she honored her birth mother by wearing something that reminded her of the mom she lost.

Learn their Tells

One of my daughters has a distinct, disconnected facial expression when a trauma episode is on its way. The first time I saw that expression after learning what it meant, I quickly had her use an essential oil blend called Rescue Remedy® and we headed off the worst of the trauma episode. Now when I see that sign, I use whatever technique is available in that moment to stop the episode or at least make it less severe. Become a student of your child. Learn his or her tells, mood changes, or expressions.

After you work through a trauma episode, take time to think it through and try to find the trigger or signs that it was coming. This knowledge will help you handle or avoid future episodes and may be helpful for other caregivers in your child's life.

Essential Oils

There are many essential oils that may be helpful for trauma. Some are for immediate use during a trauma episode and some help relieve the effects of trauma on the body over time.

Our personal favorite is Bach's Rescue Remedy®. We literally never leave home without it. I always have a bottle in the kitchen, upstairs, and in my purse. My girls are used to it now and even ask for it if they notice their trigger in time.

An essential oil blend called Release may be helpful to release the toxins left in the body by older trauma.

Body Movement for Trauma

Claudia Meyer, an occupational therapist, teaches techniques of body movement that may help break a trauma episode. I reached out to Claudia for help understanding the effects of trauma and ideas of how to help our children during a traumatic episode.

According to Claudia, trauma resets and predisposes the brain to have a narrower range of response. As this happens we are more likely to be easily triggered and to use lower brain states because they are protective. These lower brain states usually appear as fight, flight, or freeze. Movement, especially movement across the midline, supports flexibility both in movement and in the resourcefulness of the brain, freeing up our reasoning and our creativity. Crossing the midline increases communication and efficiency between brain centers to establish focus, to better capture detail, and to bring the senses together in a more coordinated way to attend to and do problem-solving. Crossing the midline and rhythmic body movements are two techniques she uses regularly.

Technique 1: Crossing the midline

Imagine a line running down the middle of your body from the top of your head to between your feet. That is your midline for this plan. The person in the trauma episode does an activity that makes an arm or leg cross the midline. We do both.

For example, kick your right leg over to the left while reaching your left arm across to the right in front of your body. Then reverse.

Back and forth, back and forth. I typically do this with my child, so we are implementing the solution together. After three or four minutes, I ask how she is feeling. If it's helping, we keep going. If not, we move on to one of our other trauma tools.

Technique 2: Bilateral Rhythmic Body Movement

To get both sides of the body moving, try marching in place, lifting your legs high. Raise your arms over your head then bring them down, tapping your hands on alternating knees. Whatever your child is comfortable with, try it. We often do this as a whole family. If one person is struggling, we get in a circle and march together, holding hands, moving continually.

I love that marching and moving includes all of us as we bond and learn how to walk alongside each other during hard times. There is nothing better I could teach my children about family than the power of sticking together and helping each other through difficult situations.

Create Felt Safety

"Felt safety" is a term in the trauma community to describe the need a child has to actually feel safe. Our children may not feel safe even when there is no danger because of events in their past, and we must look for ways to help them overcome their very real fear from past experiences.

> Children who feel safe are free to heal and become secure, trusting children.

In The Connected Child, Karyn Purvis writes, "When a child feels genuinely safe,...parts of the brain that control higher learning can operate. Children who feel safe are free to heal and become secure, trusting children. Providing an atmosphere of "felt safety" disarms the primitive brain and reduces fear. It is a critical first step toward helping your child heal and grow[7]."

The primitive brain takes over during a trauma episode. That is what we are trying to disarm with felt safety in order to reduce trauma episode frequency and intensity.

As we become students of our children, we can learn where their fear surfaces and find ways to alleviate it.

A child who was neglected when very young might fear being alone, even when we think they're old enough. A child whose few possessions were taken away or destroyed may want to hold on to everything they ever get. A child who was abused may be triggered every time someone comes close unexpectedly.

It's our job to notice these struggles and help our children overcome them. We get to do the best thing for our children, even if the world thinks we're crazy. Maybe our fourteen-year-old still doesn't stay home alone.

Maybe we let our kids hold on to a lot more things than we would like. Maybe we are incredibly careful in how we physically approach them. When we are aware of their fears, we can change our behaviors and rules to meet their needs and give them felt safety. Then they have the chance to heal, grow, and experience more joy.

The great news is that we heal from trauma. The scars may never fully disappear, but the pain and frequency of the episodes lessen. I have seen this personally in myself and my children and know it to be true with my whole heart. Our God is Jehovah-Rapha, the God who heals. "He heals the brokenhearted and binds up their wounds" (Psalm 147:3).

It's in His character and who He is. One of the core attributes of God is healer. Spiritual, emotional, and physical healing all come from His mighty and gracious hand. We pray and wait for Him to heal.

Don't give up. It will probably take longer than we want it to. We don't want our precious ones to suffer, but God is trustworthy. We can rest knowing that He is in control and will heal them in His timing.

Connections

Describe for yourself what may have caused trauma in your life and your children's lives. Look for expressions or moods in your kids that let you know a trauma episode is coming.

First Step Forward

List three trauma tools you will try when
trauma episodes come. Make note of which
ones work the best for your family.

1.

2.

3.

CHAPTER 21

The Mighty Buffalo

You might never have thought of buffalo as mighty before.

Huge, strong, imposing—definitely. But mighty? Well, that's what they are in my book.

Do you want to know why? They walk into the storm—every time. Most animals will try to avoid a storm. Maybe try to run away from it.

But the storm doesn't stop, and it doesn't get tired. Eventually, the storm overtakes the animal that keeps trying to outrun it. The animal ends up being in the storm much longer than it needs to be as it tries to stay ahead of the approaching storm.

This is what cows do. They try to run away and get caught in the storm. If the cow even simply stood still and let the storm come, it would get through the storm faster than if it ran along with the storm.

But the buffalo? No way. They're much smarter and stronger than that. They do the opposite of what most animals do.

When a storm is coming, they face it head-on. They walk into it. Oftentimes they actually charge the storm. Run at it, full force, straight into the wind, rain, or snow. No fear, no hesitation.

Buffalo attack the storm. And do you know what? They get through the storm much more quickly. By facing it head-on, they get to move through it, as it moves against them until they suddenly pop out on the other side.

What if we did the same thing? What if we stopped running away and faced our storms head-on? What if we chose courage and tenacity and walked straight into the oncoming storms? How much faster could we get to the other side where hope lives if we stopped trying to outrun the storms?

This idea was planted in my heart by my dear friend, Tara, who stood by me after my ex-husband left. She was there the day I finally told my friends in Bible study how we were living. She was one who moved closer, didn't turn away from my pain. She offered her spare room to my daughter and me the day my marriage ended. She sat with me and listened to my sorrow. She encouraged me with God's truth.

A few months later, she told me I reminded her of a buffalo. I thought maybe I should be offended; then she went on to explain about the mighty buffalo charging the storm, facing the worst, and pushing through.

I was still in the phase where getting out of bed every morning was challenging. Keeping us fed and our house in some semblance of order was like slogging through knee-deep mud. I was in the middle of sorting, separating, and packing every single item in our household, making sure I divided things fairly.

This task was too painful to ask for help with. It felt as if the sorting, the physical separating of our things into different boxes was somehow pulling us further apart emotionally. A visible end to our shared life.

As I packed each item, the truth of my situation became more and more real, like the fog slowly clearing from a field. I packed boxes at night after I put my daughter to bed. Boxes of his things that used to be ours. Those days seemed unbearable, but I kept moving and taking one more weary step.

The steps were uncertain, wobbly, but I refused to give up. And my friend noticed.

She called out the good she saw as I kept putting one foot in front of the other, even when it didn't feel like much to me.

Now I love the buffalo. I am proud to be told I am acting like a buffalo. Keep moving forward, keep pressing on. I hear her words in my head whenever a big new struggle appears. I am a mighty buffalo, and I will walk through this next storm with God by my side. I won't run in fear. I won't hide. I will face it head-on and get through it the best I can. You can, too. You can stop running away, stop being frozen with fear and uncertainty, and take your first steps forward.

I found that the struggle of facing the storm, every minute of the struggle, is worth the beauty on the other side. I could still be trudging through my days, never letting go of the past. Instead, there is laughter and joy in our home.

We play and snuggle and make each other laugh until we cry. If I had stayed locked in the grief over my past, I would have missed it all. Every giggle would be quieter; every "I love you, Mom" would be shallower, every joy would be dimmed. I could have missed this.

Facing our storms isn't easy, no matter what kind of storms they are. I'm not in any way minimizing the fear and pain you are in. God isn't either. He doesn't miss one moment of your sadness or leave you alone in it.

"You keep track of all my sorrows. You have collected all my tears in your bottle. You have recorded each one in your book" (Psalm 56:8 NLT).

He also doesn't want you to stay there. He wants you to find joy again, joy in Him and the life He has given you. It's going to take work. It's going to take prayer.

What storm are you facing today that you want to hide from? What step can you take this very minute to move forward and face the fear, face the sadness, face the unknown? You can't outrun these storms.

> There is no easy way out. There is no way around. There is only through.

I talked to someone recently who told me her storms chase her every day. That she runs away, trying to escape them. Every single day.

She's been running from them for five years. That's a long time to let the storms chase you. That's a long time to be running on empty, hoping the storms dissipate on their own.

They won't.

The storms of life don't go away unless we turn around and walk into them.

Unless we handle them and work hard to overcome them.

There is no easy way out. There is no way around. There is only through.

The beauty that awaits you on the other side is truly breathtaking. It's time to take your first step toward healing, your first step toward a bright and beautiful future.

Be like the buffalo.

Connections

What circumstances in your life are you
trying to avoid? What pain from your past
are you stuffing down instead of facing?

First Step Forward

Write down three good things you want in your
future that are worth walking into the storm for.

1.

2.

3.

CHAPTER 22

After the Storm

My friend Lauren faced her storm with unending courage.

Lauren had a difficult childhood, including an absent father and an alcoholic mother. When her boyfriend wanted to marry her when she was sixteen years old, she was thrilled.

Lauren thought she had finally found love and stability. Someone to truly count on. Her mother gave the legal approval, and Lauren was married.

Her marriage turned out nothing like the fairy tale life she had hoped for. She had a baby girl and found her husband becoming angrier and angrier. More and more abusive.

Lauren decided this was her lot in life. She stood in his anger and let it wash over her, not seeing how it was affecting their daughter.

Over several years, her husband became more controlling, not wanting her to have friends, insisting on knowing where she was at all times.

These are classic signs women are told to avoid in a relationship but often don't see until it's too late. Lauren's husband demeaned her, told her she was stupid, and slowly over time, his words found their way deep into her soul, and she began to believe them.

One day, while Lauren was baby sitting a friend's son in her home, her husband began one of his rages, and the toddler started crying. Conversely, her daughter continued playing, completely unaffected by her dad's screaming.

That was the moment that opened Lauren's eyes.

She saw that for her daughter, that environment had become normal, something she was used to and how she expected life to be. Lauren didn't want her daughter to grow up in that anger and learn it was acceptable to be treated that way. But she was also very afraid of her husband.

Lauren knew how volatile her husband was, and she was intensely scared. Scared for herself about what he would do if she tried to leave. Scared for herself and her daughter if she didn't leave. Scared knowing she didn't have anywhere to go or any way to survive on her own.

She knew what could happen if she tried to leave, that she might not survive his anger this time. She also knew this was not the way she wanted to spend the rest of her life.

Lauren wasn't willing to continue living in fear and danger. She desperately wanted a better life for herself and her child. She contacted a women's shelter and waited until they had a room available.

She planned and worked and chose just the right day. Her husband was out; she didn't know how long she had until he returned, but she packed what she could and had her mom pick her up.

Even now, several years later, when Lauren told me about those moments of escape, her fear was palpable. She told me about making sure her cell phone was off so her husband couldn't track her. She spoke of the shame she felt at going to the shelter because she didn't want to be without a home for her daughter and felt like a failure as a mom. Except she wasn't. Lauren was amazing and brave and courageous. She took a huge risk and, in doing so, gave herself the chance to start over.

Lauren worked hard to build a new life for herself and her daughter. She wasn't raised in a Christian home, but after she left her abusive husband, she found her way to God and to church. The isolation she was in during her marriage has melted away and been replaced by a loving community that has welcomed her and cares for her well.

> That's not where the story ends. Your story isn't over yet.

Lauren's situation is familiar to many single moms who have felt overwhelming oppression in their homes, who have conquered unimaginable fear to leave their homes, and who have started over. Many single moms come through to the other side of their relationships bruised, broken, hurting. But I have amazing news for you.

That's not where the story ends. Your story isn't over yet. Once the storm is over and the gentle rain at the end of it subsides, do you know what happens next?

The flowers bloom.

We are the flowers, friend. We get to bloom! We get a chance to start over and remember who we are. We get a chance to rediscover things we love, people we love, and who we want to be. And then we get to make it happen.

Lauren found her way to her new church family. She joined our single moms' group, where I met her, and eventually joined a small group. She has so many people surrounding her now. She and her new friends spend time together with their children, go on weekend getaways together, and generally share their lives. It's a whole new world of support, fun, and possibilities.

This is a great time to pick up an old hobby or try a new one—a great time to reach out to new friends and build your community. Think about things you used to love and consider if you want them back in your life.

For me, these activities ranged from the seemingly small and silly to big and adventurous. I remembered that I used to love lots of ice in my drinks, especially fun-shaped ice cubes by the handfuls. My soda tasted better when it was super cold, and I loved the clinking sound.

I had stopped using ice towards the end of my marriage and hadn't used it in years. Until one day, I really noticed how much ice my best friend used. I had been making it before her visits for several years, and it suddenly occurred to me how much I used to like ice.

The next thing I knew, I had pulled out my fun-shaped ice cube trays from IKEA and was making them just for me. Fish and heart and star-shaped ice. It's a tiny thing, but it brings me a bit of happiness every time I do it.

Then, as I was preparing for Christmas one year, I looked at my plainly wrapped packages with a single bow and recalled the hours I used to spend elaborately decorating each package and choosing the perfect paper for each gift recipient, adding piles of ribbon and curling it so it would fill the top and cascade down the sides of the presents.

For years, I didn't have the energy to care about making those presents pretty. Now I can't wait for the next chance to go over the top with ribbon to delight someone.

As I looked to expand my community, I decided to host a game day at my house. I prepared three kinds of cheese dip and chips and bought a bunch of soda and lemonade. Then I threw open the doors and invited whoever wanted to come.

Laughter filled my house, and people who wouldn't have normally known each other were becoming friends. We all had a blast.

Frankie even got a special sweatshirt just for game day that says, "savage." This girl is anything but savage! She is fun and boisterous and loves that the savage sweatshirt brings out the fun, competitive side in Rachel, one of our regular guests.

As I continue building our amazing life, I am adding more and more intentional time with my daughters. From once-a-month cooking, crafting, and game days to 20 minutes outside with our dog at the end of the day. Whatever I can do to add life and fun to our days.

You can do it, too.

Look back beyond the bad times and search for things you used to love. Give them a try and see what fits in your new life and what doesn't. Find what brings you and your kiddos joy. What makes it easier to forget the storms and move toward blooming.

Surviving the storm makes us stronger, more beautiful, and more compassionate. Surviving the storm helps us see the beauty in simple everyday things like a peaceful home, a kind word, and a full ice cube tray. Surviving the storm is something to celebrate, something to cherish. It's something to look back on with pride and say, "God and I did that together."

I can't wait to see you bloom.

Connections

What is something you loved to do in the past
that you haven't done in a long time?

First Step Forward

Make a plan to try three things you used to
enjoy or that you have wanted to try.

1.

2.

3.

CHAPTER 23

Leading Well

Most of us know the marriage sermon all too well. The one where the pastor explains how to be a godly wife and how to be a godly husband, how the two should work together in raising their family. I'm embarrassed to say that I used to skip church if I knew the sermon would be about marriage because it was too hard to listen to what should have been.

I believe in Christian marriage. I believe in forever. But that's not my story. It can never be my story. Right now, my story is about a single mom learning to lead her children well.

Survival Mode

For the first few years of this single mom life, I was in survival mode.

I loved my daughter well, and she knew it. I kept food on the table and a roof over our heads. She had adorable hand-me-down and thrift-store clothes and plenty of toys. She had a mom who loved her beyond measure, but I hadn't yet stepped into the role of leader.

Looking back, I was awkwardly the leader in my marriage. I didn't want to lead, but someone had to. I put food on the table while raising a child and trying to save a marriage. I attempted to submit to my husband, but submitting to someone who doesn't want to lead is difficult.

I was making sure life went as smoothly as possible, but I wasn't leading for the future. I was waiting to be led. After becoming a single mom, I spent several years floundering, not sure what my role should be. I grew up in church and have heard plenty of teaching on male and female roles. I learned that God designed men and women differently, with different strengths and weaknesses.

The man is to love the woman as Christ loved the Church (and gave himself up for her, Ephesians 5:25).

A woman is to submit to a godly husband's leadership (which she will be more able to do when he is leading and loving well).

But what about the single mom?

I wasn't designed to be the leader of a family. But here I am. For my children's sake, I needed to learn to step into that role and lead them well. Not be waiting for someone else to come lead us. Not wishing it wasn't my job. Stepping up and leading with confidence because that's what God calls me to do.

Yep. I am a woman, and I am called to lead.

A pastor in my church gave a sermon recently about marriage and respect in the home. I was debating about whether to go when I suddenly realized how much my daughters need to hear these lessons.

They aren't going to learn how to have a great marriage built with Christ by watching me right now.

They need to hear godly men speaking godly truths.

They need to learn what a godly relationship looks like, so they know what to wait for in their own lives.

I knew we had to go, so they wouldn't miss these important

lessons. I put up my wall to protect my heart and planned to be there for my daughters' benefit.

The sermon was built around traditional male and female roles lived out in a God-honoring way. At first, I started to shut it out, as I had planned since I didn't have a husband to submit to or be led by. Then, for the first time, God got through to my heart about this issue. I am supposed to lead. Until or unless God provides a husband, I am the leader. I started listening intently, wondering what I could learn and apply in my own home.

The pastor talked about his prayer time in the morning. He asked God what he could do to love his wife well that day. How could he lead his family better that day? He talked about God being his leader. Just like God is mine. I can do that. I can ask God how I can love my children well today. I can ask Him to make me a better leader. I can ask for wisdom and guidance in how to lead my family well.

I almost felt God sighing. A satisfied, "she finally got it" sigh.

God will lead through me, and He will lead through you, if we let Him. He knew we would be in this place, in this situation. He isn't surprised and isn't wondering what to do. He's waiting for us to finally step into the role of leader of our families—not just by putting food on the table, but truly leading them as Christ led the church. We are to teach them through our words, and by our example, how to live for Christ.

We are in Charge

God made me the overseer of my little flock, and He made you the overseer of yours. He knew this was coming, and He gave us our children on purpose. God is calling us to step up and lead our flocks well. "Keep watch over yourselves and all the flock of which the Holy Spirit has made you overseers" (Acts 20:28a).

Lead with Grace

God tells us to put our children first, to value others above ourselves. We still need to take care of ourselves, so we have the emotional and physical stamina to care for our kids, but as leaders, we are supposed to put their needs and their well-being first. To serve them in humility, not using power to control them but grace to lead them.

"Do nothing out of selfish ambition or vain conceit. Rather, in humility value others above yourselves, not looking to your own interests but each of you to the interests of the others" (Philippians 2:3-4).

Acknowledge God's Authority

Let your children know that God is truly the one in charge, that you are obeying Him in how you lead your family.

I remind my children it is their job to obey me and my job to obey God. They are learning to obey Him by learning to obey me in our home. I let them know that I am completely under the authority of Almighty God and am doing my best to follow His instructions.

One of my girls bucks against any and every rule. She can't stand the thought of obeying just because she should. She was stunned when I told her I have to follow rules, too, so I told her about the rules I follow: show up for work on time, do my job to the best of my abilities, pay my bills on time, treat others with love and compassion, and follow the rules God clearly laid out in His Word.

I want her to understand that learning to obey me is training her to obey God as a grown-up. "Keep my words and store up my commands within you. Keep my commands and you will live; guard my teachings as the apple of your eye. Bind them on your fingers; write them on the tablet of your heart" (Proverbs 7:1-3).

"Then Jesus came to them and said, 'All authority in heaven and on earth has been given to me. Therefore go and make disciples of all nations, baptizing them in the name of the Father and of the Son and of the Holy Spirit, and teaching them to obey everything I have commanded you'" (Matthew 28:18-20).

> My job is to keep walking forward in faith, following God intently, and choosing to trust Him with our future.

Seek Wise Counsel

We are not called to lead our families on our own. Not by a long shot.

Godly men who are leading their families well are seeking God first: seeking His will, His guidance, His direction. Then they lead their families in the way God instructs them to. It's the same for us. We need to be seeking God, seeking wise biblical counsel from trusted godly leaders, not trying to do this alone.

"For lack of guidance a nation falls, but victory is won through many advisers" (Proverbs 11:14).

"I will instruct you and teach you in the way you should go; I will counsel you with my loving eye on you" (Psalm 32:8).

Trust God for our Future

There are days I would like to know what God is planning. This whole "lighting up one step at a time" thing gets old. I want to see the whole picture. I want to see how He is planning to redeem this. I want a glimpse of the great big, amazing future he has planned for us. But then I guess it wouldn't take much faith to follow Him, would it?

My job is to keep walking forward in faith, following God intently, and choosing to trust Him with our future. Because He is infinitely trustworthy and infinitely good, I can do that.

"'For my thoughts are not your thoughts, neither are your ways my ways,' declares the Lord. 'As the heavens are higher than the earth, so are my ways higher than your ways and my thoughts than your thoughts'" (Isaiah 55:8-9).

"And we know that in all things God works for the good of those who love him, who have been called according to his purpose" (Romans 8:28).

Seek out Examples of Godly Men

If men are in short supply in our everyday lives, we need to be intentional in seeking out godly men for our kids to see.

I am in a life group at church that is for parents of teens. We share our concerns and hopes and seek to apply Scripture to our parenting together. Through our studies and fun times as a group, I have seen these men live out their faith through words and actions. Whenever we have the chance to spend time as families, I make sure to be there. My girls get up-close examples of godly men working, serving, and having fun.

You may find these men at church, through friends and neighbors, or at school. Annie's son has a big brother through Big Brothers Big Sisters of America. He has been with his big brother for about six years now, and his big brother has shown up for him, time and time again. If you naturally have a lack of godly men in your lives, seeking them out will be so helpful for your kids.

Teach Them to Pray

I remember being afraid to pray in front of others when I was younger. I was embarrassed and worried I would say something silly. I want my girls to be confident in their prayers, knowing the God who loves them never judges the quality of their words, He just listens and answers.

I want them to be unafraid, to talk to God like they would talk to their best friends. Our friends from Uganda came to visit, and I saw my Ugandan friend guide his children in prayer. He told his son to pray before our meal. Then he quietly and gently told him what to pray for.

Thank God for the food and the preparer of the food, thank Him for all the blessings we saw today, ask for His hand to be upon us as we continue our time together. And his son prayed. He led his daughter the same way the next night.

It was lovely. It was kind, gentle, and humble. Simply teaching them to pray.

I started a simple prayer time with my girls, asking them if there is anything or anyone they want to pray for. I'll keep leading until they want to step in and pray on their own, but for now, they still get to learn how to pray and see prayers answered.

Set the Tone

As the parents, we set the tone in our homes. If I am ornery and whiney, you can bet my kids will follow suit. If I face difficult circumstances with grace and trust, my girls will learn that, too.

We had a hard morning yesterday. Emotions ran high and deep struggles were discussed. After we had a chance to settle from the stress, I started acting playful. Said silly things, made my girls laugh. A serious time was needed; we had to face and talk about what was happening. The fun, light-hearted time afterward was just as necessary.

How we as moms respond to life sets the tone for our entire home. We can join in the chaos and anger and stress when it arises, or we can seek to diffuse it. We'll never be perfect, but we get to keep trying.

Press on No Matter What

When we have given all we have, when we have corrected the behavior for the millionth time, when our kids are struggling with science homework while dinner burns on the stove and wet laundry is forgotten in the washing machine, DO NOT QUIT.

God sees you. He knows how hard you are working, and He knows you are tired. Don't give up. God is working behind the scenes. He is up to something even when we can't see it. Keep holding on and moving forward every single day.

"Let us not become weary in doing good, for at the proper time we will reap a harvest if we do not give up" (Galatians 6:9).

Being raised to follow well didn't make the transition to leader of my family easy. Knowing that's what God expects from me right now makes it necessary. I am so grateful that God worked patiently and persistently until He broke through the stereotypes that I fought so hard to keep. Stereotypes that didn't serve my family well at all.

When I finally chose to step into the role of leader of my family, God was able to use me in new and beautiful ways. I'm grateful that He leads me well. He's waiting to lead you, too.

Connections

Have you stepped into the role as the leader in your home?
Is there an area in which you need to lead more fully?

First Step Forward

Write down three ways you are going to seek
to be a better leader in your home.

1.

2.

3.

NOT OVER YET

CHAPTER 24

Speaking Truth Over Yourself & Your Children

Trauma literally changes the connections in the brain.

Depending on the level of trauma and when it occurred, it may even change how the brain is wired to begin with. Fascinating (and troubling) studies show pictures of brain activity in a typical brain and in a brain that has experienced trauma. The images are striking. While the healthy brain shows colorful areas in the temporal lobes indicating lots of activity, the brain that has experienced trauma or abuse has large black areas in the temporal lobes indicating dormancy[8].

It would be so easy to get caught up in those images, to see how our brains have been changed, and to feel hopeless. But we serve a great God. Nothing is hopeless with Him.

In fact, God designed us to heal. He designed the brain to be capable of making new connections, of being rewired. Dr. Caroline Leaf has thirty-eight years of experience in the fields of mental health and neuroscience. She describes neuroplasticity as "the brain structurally changing as thoughts are growing" and says that because the brain is neuroplastic, "it can change, it always changes, and it is never too late to change[9]." We get to direct the way in which it changes.

Dr. Leaf explains it this way. "True transformation requires mind management strategies to rewire neural pathways...We can methodically use our mind to take advantage of neuroplasticity to rework our neural circuitry, managing and improving a variety of mental and physical states, even if we have very dysfunctional brain networks and physiology from toxic thoughts and trauma[10]!"

Neuroplasticity allows us to rewire our minds through attentive action. It won't happen on its own. People who have lived through trauma may have brains that are rewired by those incidents and need healing.

Dr. Rick Hanson of Berkley's Greater Good Science Center says, "Intense, prolonged, or repeated mental/neural activity—especially if it is conscious—will leave an enduring imprint in neural structure, like a surging current reshaping a riverbed. In the saying in neuroscience: Neurons that fire together, wire together. Mental states become neural traits. Day after day, your mind is building your brain[11]."

We see it in kids who have been verbally abused. After a while, they believe all the bad things said about themselves and lose hope. The same is true in reverse. Speaking truth and life over ourselves and our children can rewire our brains to make connections that weren't made because of early childhood trauma or that were broken later in life.

We start by practicing our thoughts. We take control of our thoughts. We learn to face the anxiety and pain from our past and actively work to replace those thoughts.

New York Times best-selling author Jon Acuff calls them soundtracks. He worked with a researcher to discover how those soundtracks affect our lives and how we can change the ones that are harmful. His research showed we need to retire our old soundtracks, replace them with true, helpful soundtracks, and repeat those new soundtracks until they are natural parts of how we think. Retire, replace, repeat[12].

I decided to give this a try. One of my girls has been through so much. I couldn't find anything that helped her deal with the root of her trauma since she was too afraid to face those memories.

No amount of telling her how great life would be on the other side of healing made a difference. She couldn't see the hope. She couldn't feel the hope. And if someone doesn't have hope for their future, why would they even try?

I was praying and seeking wisdom. What else could I possibly do to help her? Then I remembered those studies and Acuff's research and began speaking truth over her as often as I could.

When she faced another struggle, I would wait until the storm calmed and then ask her what started it. Together we can usually figure it out. And we often find the struggles are from lies she believes about herself or me. I acknowledge the pain and the lies and then expose the lies with the truth.

> Like a torch in a darkened cave, the truth enters and changes everything.

Like a torch in a darkened cave, the truth enters and changes everything. I tell her the truths she is living in now. She is safe, she is loved, she is valued. I am on her side. And slowly, those truths sink in and change her heart and heal her mind.

I took it a step further to help her fight off the lies before they attack again. I wrote out words of truth. Words that would speak life and love over her. I made it fun and printed it out. I put her favorite colors and designs on it, so she would see the love I put into it. Then I asked her to read it out loud to herself in the mirror every morning.

> I am safe. I am brave. I am filled with the never-ending strength of God.

> I am chosen. I am wanted. I am loved by my mom, my sister, and the King of Kings.

> I am kind, thoughtful, and truly care about others.

> I will tell the truth. I will obey. I will let my best self shine through.

> I have a big, bright, amazing future and I am going to go get it.

Slowly and surely, the lies are being weeded out and the truth is taking root. All of us need this. We all have lies we have lived with for way too long. Something we were told in childhood or as teenagers. Something we were called during our marriages. Lies that have no place in our amazing futures. It's time to dig them out and replace them with beautiful truths.

Connections

What lies do you believe about yourself?
What lies might your children believe about
themselves that are holding them back?

First Step Forward

Write out three good truths about yourself
and read them out loud every day.

1.

2.

3.

NOT OVER YET

CHAPTER 25

Growing Great Kids

Raising children well doesn't happen by accident. One of our biggest concerns as single moms is how having only one parent at home will affect our kids. Will they grow up to beat the statistics? How will they learn what a good relationship looks like? Where will they see a godly example of how a husband should treat a wife? If we are purposeful and careful, we can raise amazing kids despite what the statistics say.

My cousin married a man who was raised by a single mom. His dad wasn't around at all during his childhood. And this man is the most amazing husband and father I can imagine. Supportive and caring towards his wife, present and engaged with his children.

He is an incredible example for my girls.

I love when they get to see that couple in action. His sisters are equally kind, caring, and successful. I know without a doubt that it is possible to raise amazing kids who overcome the challenges of having only one parent in their everyday lives. Some key areas need our special attention.

Protection

Our kids need us to be their gatekeeper and protector. I have a filter on our internet so inappropriate and dangerous content is much less likely to enter our home. I also have the rule that my girls can't be on the internet if I'm not in the room.

Malicious content and destructive people are everywhere, and they aren't going to get to my girls if I have anything to say about it.

There are many things in life I have no control over. No way to protect my children. But what happens in this home? That is in my control. And I will make sure that they are loved and safe and cared for and treated well in this home.

Some single moms have told me that they don't see the point in enforcing strict protective rules, since the rules don't apply in the other parent's home.

It doesn't matter.

Yes, it's harder to enforce the rules if they only apply in your home, but it's still worth it. You can still explain the reasons to your kids and let them know you want them to be safe. They may even surprise you and want to follow the rules elsewhere. Whether or not they do, we can't control what happened earlier in their lives, and we can't control everything that happens when they're not home.

My girls' homework is almost entirely done on a computer, which makes this rule a bit confusing for them. Once they are set up in a particular program, say for math, I will leave the room and trust them to stay in that program. They can do their work and submit assignments without me present. But if they are doing research on the internet? Not a chance.

Even with me there, we've seen inappropriate things, which I cover quickly and close the window. It shouldn't be like this. I wish we could trust that there is so much good in the world that our kids will be safe all the time. That isn't the world we live in. And since we know it, it's our job to protect them as much as we can.

Here, inside the walls of our homes, our kids can be safe.

Discipline

In my house, no one likes discipline. Not the one receiving it and not the one giving it.

I would much rather have the day run smoothly without any incidents requiring discipline. But there it is. Another lie; another angry outburst.

Listen, our kids have lived through a lot, and they're only kids. Their brains won't be fully developed until they're in their early twenties, so we are going to have issues to deal with. Holding it together is sometimes beyond their control.

I do my best to correct in kindness and love, even in the face of anger. And let me tell you, I fail a lot. I struggle to stay calm and kind when confronted with intense anger.

One of my favorite verses to pray in this situation is Psalm 141:3: "Set a guard over my mouth, Lord; keep watch over the door of my lips."

God has helped me keep my mouth shut on more than one occasion. It's usually best to let the moment pass and talk about it later when tempers have subsided. No one can think clearly and have a productive conversation when their emotions have taken over.

I know it's not fun to be the one to discipline all the time, especially if the child doesn't get any discipline in the other home. But our kids need us to give them strong boundaries.

They need to know what is expected of them, and they need to be held to that standard.

I used to be pretty easy on my oldest daughter since we were living alone, and I felt such guilt over her not having her dad around. Now I see that won't serve her well later in life. She needs to take responsibility for her actions and control of herself in order to be a fully functioning adult. So, I changed course and began holding her more accountable for her choices and giving her jobs to do around the house. Little by little, teaching her new skills and watching responsibility grow. When we see something that needs to be different, it's never too late to change directions.

Laughter: The Best Parenting

Take a breath. Your child may be acting completely impossible. There may be tantrums and attitudes and disobedience. And yes, those things require consequences. But sometimes, your child just needs you.

The consequences can wait. It can be so hard for our grown-up hearts. At least it is for mine.

One particular day one of my girls was making terrible choices, one after the other. I wanted it to be bedtime already!

We had only a few minutes at the end of the day, and I did not feel like trying anymore. I wanted to discipline, send her to bed, and sit alone in peace. Instead, I took a deep breath, prayed, and asked her if she wanted to play a card game. She was shocked but said yes.

I fought my feelings of pride and wanting an apology and pushed through as best I could. After a few minutes, I found myself playing, truly playing with her, being melodramatic, using funny voices. And then she laughed.

Laughed.

I had fought so hard for that moment. And God was incredibly gracious and gave it to me.

He softened her heart, and softened mine, and we got to end the night on a good note.

Be FOR Your Child

I am crazy about my kids. There is no one in the world who wants to see them healthy and joyful more than I do. No matter what they face, they know that I am on their side. I am for them. I am cheering them on. Even when I am guiding or correcting them, they know I am for them. I bet you feel the same way about yours.

When we have moments where I can see them teetering on the edge of a bad decision and they catch themselves and do the right thing? Wow, do I celebrate. I jump up and down, I hoot and holler until they think I am completely looney. But I also see the look. That little smile that says they are so glad their choice made Mom go nuts. Totally worth it!

Raising our children well takes time and intention. Holding the boundaries to protect and guide them will be absolutely worth the effort in the end.

When I am overwhelmed and exhausted, I ask God to give me His strength to be the mom He wants me to be. When I remember to ask Him, He never lets me down. He calls us to train up our children in the way they should go; so, when they are old, they will not depart from it, (Proverbs 22:6). Our job is to do the training; His job is everything else.

Since He calls us to do it, He will certainly provide all we need to make it happen.

Eventually as our children grow, they will separate from us, as they should. No matter what the future holds or what decisions they make, we want to be able to rest knowing we did our best to raise them well. To guide them, teach them and protect them as only a mom can.

Connections
Is there something you want to change about your parenting, something that needs improvement?

First Step Forward
Write explanations for a few household rules in a way that your children understand how they are being protected and trained for the future.

1.

2.

3.

CHAPTER 26

Always Listen

I want my girls to talk to me about everything. For every major decision they'll have to make in life, I want them to know I am willing to listen and advise if asked. Always.

I tell them this over and over, and I follow it up with action. I will answer any question they ask at an age-appropriate level. They know I will never ever, in my life, lie to them. I might say that I will tell them when they're older, but I won't lie.

They know they can trust me.

If we want this relationship with our kids, we need to become the world's best listeners. They need to know that they will always be listened to and heard. They need to know that we will give them space to share and not be judged. Guided and loved and directed, but not judged. They need to know we are the safest place in the world for them.

The hardest feelings and thoughts to talk about seem to be the ones that most need to be shared. I have only recently gotten brave enough to tell parts of my story to my closest friends. And I learned that finally saying these things out loud took away a lot of their power. I am teaching my girls to talk about it. Whatever "it" may be.

One of my girls came home from school one day and told me she was sad and scared because of a video they had watched in social studies. Her voice was soft, low, and she could barely raise her eyes to look into mine.

My heart ached for her. I told her how proud I was of her for being willing and able to tell me how she felt. She struggles in this area, and that alone was a huge accomplishment.

I asked her what the video was about, and she wanted me to watch it so she wouldn't have to describe it. At that moment, I knew it was important to her healing for her to do the work herself. To find the words and explain why the video affected her so. I asked her if she could tell me about it instead.

With bated breath, I watched her search to find the words and the strength. She was so brave. She took a deep breath and told me what it was about and that she couldn't imagine why that was so frightening for her.

I could.

Shuddering inwardly at the memory it was triggering from her past, I gently told her what I thought it was, then I wrapped my arms firmly around her and held her safely while we prayed. I felt the bond between us tighten with my hug.

When they share their hearts with us, we need to take them very seriously. One of the great privileges of being called mom is being able to offer constant love.

Being a single mom makes it even more important (and challenging) since there is no one else to pick up the slack. No matter how tired we are or how many chores are waiting, we need to listen to our kids.

Guiding their hearts should always come before cleaning on our to-do lists.

I check in with my girls often, asking them about their friends, their days at school. We eat dinner together most nights and ask each other for our favorite and least favorite parts of the day. The conversations that develop when my girls start sharing are beautiful. And the days they don't have much to say? I figure something else out. I might ask them a crazy question, like if they would prefer to ride an elephant or a giraffe. Or maybe if they could go anywhere in the world right now, where would it be.

Yes, Disney World is the most common answer.

Recently I started asking them what I could pray for them. Hearing their answers teaches me so much about them. I was told about a friend whose dog died and asked to pray for her because she was crying in class. I learned about other friends who are struggling with sickness.

As busy as our lives are, no matter how long our list of tasks is, let's lean in whenever our children want to talk. Let's be the safe space for them to share their hearts without judgment, so they will always know we are a safe place for them to land.

Connections
What are some things that distract you from your kids?

First Step Forward
Set aside a time to listen to your kids and let them know
you want to hear anything they want to share.

CHAPTER 27

Get Off the Tilt-a-Whirl

Do you remember the Tilt-a-Whirl? Every time we went to a carnival when I was little, I immediately raced towards the Tilt-a-Whirl, with its cars shaped like big half-eggs.

As the ride begins, you slowly start moving up and down big hills, and with each rise and fall, the car swings from side to side. As the ride goes faster and faster, so does the swinging until it's going full force and the entire car is spinning in circles while going up and down around the track. My sister, dad, and I would get squished together as the car swung around in circles, and if we all leaned hard to one side, we could make it spin even faster. I loved it!

Wanting to share this favorite childhood experience with my daughter, I decided to take her to a fun little amusement park and was thrilled that she was tall enough to ride the Tilt-a-Whirl!

We waited in line and got in our car. The ride started slowly, and I was watching her anticipation. Then we started spinning.

Let me tell you, the Tilt-a-Whirl was a completely different experience at thirty-eight years old than it was at seven.

Almost immediately, I became nauseous. Seriously nauseous. As we spun faster and faster, I wondered if my face was actually turning green like in the cartoons I watched as a kid. I caught the eye of the attendant and silently pleaded for the ride to stop.

But on and on we spun.

I survived to the end of the ride and then had to sit down for two hours. Two hours sitting at a picnic table while my daughter and her dad went on rides and had fun. I couldn't even walk. It literally took an entire week until my body and head felt normal again. I have never been so physically off-kilter in my life.

For some of us, that's what our marriages were like in the end. One long Tilt-a-Whirl ride that wouldn't end. Getting dizzier and dizzier, more and more off-balance until life was almost unmanageable, and we were left sitting there waiting for stability to return. We may not have had control over the ending. We may have been at the mercy of the ride operator to finally stop the ride, so we could start regaining our balance, our ability to move forward, and stand on our own two feet.

So, here's the thing. Don't get back on that ride.

Ever.

Take all the time you need to heal physically, emotionally, and mentally. Wait until you are separated from the relationship for long enough that you can look at it logically, with as little emotion as possible.

Once we have lived in a difficult relationship for long enough, we have often adapted to it. Maybe it started so gradually that we didn't even see the problems until they were overwhelming.

Maybe we saw them in the first few months or even in the first few days after saying "I do," but were committed to marriage, so we stayed anyway.

Look for the signs that you may have missed early in the relationship and promise yourself that you won't miss them again. Surround yourself with people who will speak truth into your life. People who will strongly, lovingly tell you when they see a problem or have a concern about someone you are interested in dating.

Be willing to listen to them. And remember that once you are off-kilter, it's hard to see straight and make good decisions.

Susan's Story

Susan says that her ex-husband changed almost immediately after the wedding. Suddenly she didn't know who he was anymore. He had been hiding his true self from her and continued to hide it from her family for years.

She separated from him a few times and asked her church for help, but she always went back. Susan never got far enough away to regain her balance and see the situation clearly until her family stepped in and discovered the full extent of what she was living in and went and rescued her.

It took years for her to see clearly what had happened and that it wasn't OK. It took years for her to begin rewriting the words in her head. The untruths about herself that she had been told day after day, year after year.

Other women are told that it will be different this time, that he has changed, but way too often, those words are empty. There is absolutely a time for forgiveness and to possibly consider reconciliation. However, remember that being told things will be different, and actually seeing different actions and behaviors are two very different things. Actions matter far more than words. A tree is known by its fruit and a person by their actions.

"For no good tree bears bad fruit, nor does a bad tree bear good fruit" (Luke 6:43).

You cannot change someone else. They have to want to change, and it will take a herculean effort for them to change.

Really, it takes God. God can change a heart, and without Him, a heart (and thus, actions) are not likely to change.

If you are considering reconciliation, please get advice and counseling from wise, godly people first. Reconciliation would most likely require individual and couples counseling or other outside intervention. Don't put yourself back in danger, simply hoping things will be different.

Once you get off that ride, don't get back on.

Whether you are considering trying to reconcile the previous relationship or are interested in a new relationship, make sure you take the time and do the work so you don't end up in a similar situation again.

> Once you get off that ride, don't get back on.

Don't let the drama or untruth or sins of another person pull you back onto the ride that overtakes every part of you. Walk away and get the help you need for healing to begin. Walk away and learn the truth about what God says about you and speak that over yourself every day until those are the words that ring in your ears—until those are the words that lead you through each day and guide every step of your journey.

Connections

What characteristics do you find attractive in a man that might tempt you to get back on the Tilt-a-Whirl?

First Step Forward

List three friends or family members who will help hold you accountable to wait for God's best for you and tell them you want their help.

1.

2.

3.

NOT OVER YET

CHAPTER 28

Before Next Time

When I first became a single mom years ago, I had no intention of ever dating again. The last few years of my marriage had been almost unbearable, filled with so much pain, so much neglect, so little peace. I didn't want to risk that happening ever again. I had been in survival mode for a long time, and I felt unsure of how to get back into the life I had been missing. I wanted to stay in my little cocoon, focused on my daughter.

I knew I needed help. Needed healing. Needed someone who had been through this before and could help light the path ahead of me. So, I went through DivorceCare®.

DivorceCare® is a divorce recovery support group by Church Initiative. There are 13 weekly meetings with video lessons and studies to do on your own. The lessons include Deep Hurt, Road to Recovery, Anger and Financial and Legal Issues. The goal is to provide comfort and hope on the path to recovery after divorce.

There is so much brokenness when a marriage ends, no matter how it ends. I watched the videos, did the home-work, and went to every meeting. I knew that no human relationship could provide the healing I needed. I turned to God to be my everything.

During those dark and lonely days, I learned to lean into Him and listen to His voice. I learned how to walk through each day with Christ as my companion. He was healing me, day by day.

As I grew closer to Christ, I felt Him sweetening what had been such a bitter time. I began to see with new eyes what He was doing in my life, trusting He would use this struggle for my good and His glory. Knowing He wouldn't waste a second of it. The struggle pushed me so close to Him that I even found myself a little bit grateful for it.

DivorceCare® suggests staying single for one year for every four years of marriage. For me, that would mean three-and-a-half years of singleness. At first, I was almost happy about the long wait. I felt strengthened by the commitment I was making, certain it was the right step for me. It also gave me an excuse not to have to open myself up to possible hurt again—a wise and protective move all in one.

I have watched women jumping into another relationship soon after one ended, and I have yet to see a good outcome. Their stomachs are still flipping from the tilt-a-whirl, and they are suddenly jumping in line for another round.

Loneliness can be intense enough that we want companionship. Any companionship.

Maybe we don't see the truth about ourselves anymore, don't have hope, and don't feel worthy of a good man.

Maybe we started to believe what people said about us.

Maybe we don't see our value in Christ anymore but are looking through the darkly tinted glasses of someone who couldn't see our worth.

Any one of these struggles can make us think we have to settle for anyone who will have us. Especially if we believe that a godly man wouldn't want us after all we have been through. For our good and for the good of our children, we cannot afford to believe those lies and stay in that place.

We have to remember God's mercy and grace will cover all of our past. We have to fight for our own hearts and our children's hearts. We have to let Christ set the standards for the next relationship.

> Now is the time to set the bar high. Crazy high. Olympic-athlete-on-the-high-jump-high.

Setting the Bar High

Jennifer, a single mom I know, was told by her friends that she couldn't be picky anymore because she had two kids. Nothing could be further from the truth. She needs to be pickier than ever! She is making choices now that will affect both her and her children's hearts for years to come.

Now is the time to set the bar high. Crazy high. Olympic-athlete-on-the-high-jump-high.

And here's a good place to start: Soak yourself in God's truth. Seek out what He says about you. Jeremiah 29:13-14 became a treasured Bible passage for me. "'You will seek Me and find Me when you seek me with all your heart. I will be found by you,'" declares the Lord."

I wanted to seek God and God alone with all my heart. Once His truths became rooted in my heart, and God worked on healing me from my past, I found myself yearning for love again—for someone to walk this road with me, to lead my daughters and me well.

I want this for my children as much as for myself. I want them to see what a godly marriage looks like up close and how a good man should treat them. That perspective has changed what I am looking for in a potential husband.

My Future Man List

I don't know about you, but I am ready for the love of a good man.

Loneliness could easily fool me about a man's goodness (at least for a little while). I am taking steps to make sure that doesn't happen.

I encourage all the single moms I meet to make a list of what they are looking for in a future husband. Make it before you get asked on a single date. Before you are interested. Before next time. And don't change it for ANY MAN.

If he doesn't meet the list, he doesn't get to know the wonder that is you. The right man, the one God has planned for you, will absolutely be worth waiting for. He will be beyond all you can ask or imagine.

Laminate your list, etch it in stone, do some skywriting. Do whatever you have to do to make sure you stick to the list. Find a dear friend to hold your list and help you stay accountable to what you are looking for.

Here's a sample from my list:
1. Non-Negotiables
   Completely sold out for Christ
   Loves my girls as his very own
   Thoroughly kind
   Truthful

Faithful

Compassionate

2. Super Important

   In a group of godly men (for accountability)

   Confident, humble leader

   Financially stable

   Wants to make a difference in the world

3. Wouldn't it be Cool If...?

   Wants to dance with me in the kitchen

   Is taller than me

   Likes to watch movies

   Kills all the spiders for us

Honestly? I am so ready to retire as the Chief Spider Killer. And Mouse Trap Disposer. I may throw away reusable mouse traps because I can't stand to empty them. And I certainly can't use the cheap wooden ones with the snap that make me see the destruction I've caused.

I have more than paid my dues in these areas, and I'm ready to hand over the titles.

The Non-Negotiable list is exactly what it says. I will not date a man if I know he doesn't meet those requirements. I know it may take a few dates to learn all of that, but I will not give my heart to a man who doesn't fit my list.

The Super Important section holds characteristics that are not necessarily deal-breakers, but he should meet most of them.

The Wouldn't It Be Cool If list is exactly that. My daydreams. Things that would add joy to my life. And honestly, I think God's going to meet them all. The whole list, including my Wouldn't It Be Cool Ifs. If a man is going to love me well, he will love me enough to dance with me in the kitchen.

My girls have been asking me to meet someone for a while now. They would really like me to get married, so there is a dad living in the house with us. I tell them if that's what God wants, He will send the right guy. And if not, we'll be fine exactly as we are. And then I let them dream.

When they were young, I thought I had to keep any relationship completely separate from them. I don't want them to get hurt or disappointed again. Not if I can keep them from it. I certainly plan on not telling them much about my dates, and they won't meet anyone until I know he could be the one God sent.

But one day, I realized what an amazing opportunity I have to teach them what to look for in a mate. I shared my list. We talked about each item and why it's important to me. Later that night, one of my girls asked if she could write a list of what she wants in a dad. Of course! It was one of those moments when I held my breath and listened with all of my heart to hear all of hers.

Non-Negotiable:
1. He has to be OK with crazy. We can get pretty wacky in our house. I responded with, Wouldn't it be cool if he wasn't just "OK" with crazy but actually enjoyed talking in silly accents with us??
2. He has to love animals. Obviously.
3. He has to like doing crafts. We can dream, right?

Her list went on. And when she was done, this is what I heard. She really wants to be loved well. She wants a man who will build her up and remind her how cool she is. One who will take all her big personality and uniqueness and claim her as his own. She wants another grown-up to love her.

That is at the top of my prayer list. Lord, please send a man to love all three of us well. A man to be a true partner to me, a man to protect us, a man to celebrate life with us. I pray this often. I want my girls to be loved by a dad who sets their bar high by how well he loves them.

And if God never sends him? We'll be fine.

God never promised me a husband. He promised me He would always be faithful. He will be my provider. He will be my comforter. He will be my all in all. I am not waiting for a man to arrive.

I am living each day as if he isn't coming, while fully hoping that he will. I am raising my girls right now to know that they are capable and beautiful and full of godly character. I am teaching them that while we would like God to provide a man for our family, we don't need Him to.

God will never leave us, so we'll be fine either way. And so will you.

Connections
Are there any red flags you can see in past relationships, looking back on them now? What are some of your dreams for a future relationship?

First Step Forward
Make your list of what you are looking for in a partner and share it with one trusted friend who will keep you accountable.

CHAPTER 29

In the Waiting

"So when he heard that Lazarus was sick, he stayed where he was two more days... So then he told them plainly, 'Lazarus is dead, and for your sake, I am glad I was not there, so that you may believe. But let us go to him'" (John 11:6, 14).

At first glance, I think John 11:6 is one of the strangest verses in the Bible. Jesus heard his beloved friend was incredibly ill, so he waited two more days to go see him. Lazarus had likely died while the messenger was going to find Jesus, then Jesus waited two more days before beginning his journey to Lazarus.

By the time Jesus reached the home of his dear friends, Lazarus had been dead for four days. Four days of his sisters, Mary and Martha, mourning the loss of their brother. Four days of the community knowing Lazarus was dead and mourning with the family.

It's bizarre to imagine Jesus waiting. He loved this family. They were dear friends, and we hear several accounts of their friendship in the Bible. They were close enough for Mary to scold Jesus when He arrived after Lazarus' death, telling Him that Lazarus wouldn't have died if He had come sooner.

Jesus had healed so many people. Way more than we know. He healed the woman who had bled for twelve years by her believing and simply touching his garment. He healed Jairus' daughter, who died while Jesus was on his way to her. He gave the blind man his sight and healed the leper.

> He delayed because he loved them. Because he had a greater plan and a greater lesson to teach them.

And yet, when his dear friend was dying, he waited. Which meant they waited. Mary, Martha, and Lazarus waited for healing that didn't come. At least, it didn't come when they wanted it to.

They wanted to see Lazarus healed immediately and back to normal. They wanted Jesus to show up and fix it like they knew he could. Instead, he waited. Not out of callousness or indifference. He waited because He had a better plan. He knew they would suffer for a few days, and He knew that in exchange for their suffering, they would learn about resurrection and redemption in a manner that would far outweigh the short-term suffering.

He delayed because he loved them, because he had a greater plan and a greater lesson to teach them. They got to see, beyond any doubt, that Jesus healed Lazarus. Not just healed, but actually restored him to life when he was already long gone.

Jesus' power got to be on full display in front of those who knew He was God, those who trusted Him and loved Him. They got a front row seat to an amazing display of His majesty. And those who didn't know Jesus? The ones who were mourning with Mary and Martha but weren't following Jesus' teaching or acknowledging Him as Savior? Well, they got to witness His power first-hand, His ability to do what no mere human could possibly do. They witnessed a miracle they couldn't deny.

If Lazarus had been healed before he died, the people could say he had just gotten better on his own, with whatever treatment they were using. Once he had been dead for four days, that argument wouldn't hold water. When Lazarus was restored to life here on earth, there could be no question that Jesus had divine power. No question that He actually was God.

Lazarus' death and resurrection showed God's power in a way no other miracle could.

Is He keeping you waiting, too?

Are you calling out to Him and wondering what in the world He is waiting for? Do you see what looks like a great solution if He would just do it? The fact that He is keeping you waiting doesn't mean He doesn't love you. It doesn't mean you've done something wrong. Sometimes He delays because He sees so much more than we do, and He has bigger and better plans.

Trust Him in the Wait

We can choose to wait well. To fully lean into His faithfulness and trust Him no matter how long He delays. Trust is a lot like love, an action, not a feeling. Sometimes it happens by sheer force of will.

On one particularly hard day, during a particularly hard time, I decided it was time to trust no matter how I felt. To trust in God's character, who He is, His faithfulness, His steadfast love, even though I didn't feel it.

I started saying it out loud, softly. "I will trust you." "I will trust you." "I will trust you." Slowly, I got a little louder, a little stronger willing myself to choose trust even if my circumstances looked like that was a crazy decision because, with God, it's never a crazy decision to trust Him. It's actually the only decision that fully makes sense. It took several minutes and a great big act of my will and God's grace for my words to change from "I will trust you" to "I trust you."

And that change changes everything. Choosing to trust in His almighty hand to comfort, provide, heal, and protect shifts our perspective. Trusting in His timing and His plan gives us a sure footing on any path. Knowing He personally will restore us and make us strong gives us hope for our future.

"And the God of all grace, who called you to his eternal glory in Christ, after you have suffered a little while, will himself restore you and make you strong, firm and steadfast" (1 Peter 5:10).

Connections

What are you waiting for in your life that you want God to do? How can you be faithful in the waiting?

First Step Forward

Find and write out three verses about trusting God that are meaningful to you.

1.

2.

3.

CHAPTER 30

You are Beloved

I talk a lot about how loved you are. Mostly because it's so very true, and I know you may not feel that way. Not being loved by the one human who legally committed to love us forever can deal a major blow to how we see ourselves.

It's hard to believe we are loveable when the one who knew us best stopped loving us. If we continue looking at love as a feeling, we will continue feeling inadequate, unlovable, unworthy.

And it's simply not true.

Love is an action. I have heard and read that a lot lately, until it almost doesn't mean anything anymore. So, let me say it again. Take a deep breath and really listen. Listen with your soul.

Love is an action.

Love is a commitment that should be actively lived out.

If someone committed to loving you forever, no matter what, and then walked away, it doesn't mean you are unlovable. They may have struggles they have never dealt with. They may not have committed like you did. They may not understand that love is an action and a choice, regardless of how a person feels in the day-to-day of life.

To remind you of how very loved you are, we're going straight to the source. Get some coffee or chocolate. Get in your favorite chair. Settle in. If you belong to God, take some time to read His words and know He says them about you.

You Are Loved

"The Lord appeared to us in the past, saying: 'I have loved you with an everlasting love; I have drawn you with unfailing kindness'" (Jeremiah 31:3).

"But you, O Lord, are a compassionate and gracious God, slow to anger, abounding in love and faithfulness" (Psalm 86:15).

"Oh, give thanks to the Lord, for He is good, for His steadfast love endures forever! Let the redeemed of the Lord say so, whom He has redeemed from trouble" (Psalm 107:1-2 ESV).

"The Lord, your God, is with you, the Mighty Warrior who saves. He will take great delight in you; in His love, He will no longer rebuke you, but will rejoice over you with singing" (Zephaniah 3:17).

"Your love, LORD, reaches to the heavens, your faithfulness to the skies. Your righteousness is like the highest mountains, your justice like the great deep." (Psalm 36:5-6).

"Give thanks to the Lord, for He is good, for His steadfast love endures forever" (Psalm 136:1 ESV).

"For great is His love toward us, and the faithfulness of the Lord endures forever" (Psalm 117:2).

Now do you believe God loves you? The word "love" appears 686 times in the New International Version of the Bible. God clearly wanted us to understand that He not only IS love but that He lives out love. His steadfast love endures forever. Not until He doesn't feel like it anymore. Not until He gets tired of us. Not until we do something He won't forgive. Forever. Always. For all eternity. He is the love we can count on for the rest of our lives.

> He is the love we can count on for the rest of our lives.

No matter what any human has said or done, no matter what we have said or done, God's love for us endures forever.

You Are Holy

"But now he has reconciled you by Christ's physical body through death to present you holy in His sight, without blemish and free from accusation— if you continue in your faith, established and firm, and do not move from the hope held out in the gospel" (Colossians 1:22-23).

"Therefore, as God's chosen people, holy and dearly loved, clothe yourselves with compas-

sion, kindness, humility, gentleness, and patience"
(Colossians 3:12).

"He has saved us and called us to a holy life—not
because of anything we have done but because of
His own purpose and grace" (2 Timothy 1:9).

We are not waiting to become holy once Christ returns. We
have already been made holy by believing in Christ and His
atoning sacrifice for our sins. We are certainly far from perfect
while living in this far from perfect world. But God doesn't see
our imperfections and sins when He looks on us. He sees us
covered in Christ's righteousness.

He calls us to a holy life, and He helps us live it out, purely
through His grace.

The thought of His grace toward us, the thought that He
can look on us and see Christ's righteousness covering us, the
thought that we stand holy before Him now should bring us to
our knees with gratitude and completely change the way we
see ourselves.

We get to live in the freedom that His incomparable
grace provides.

You Are Chosen

"But you are a chosen people, a royal priesthood,
a holy nation, God's special possession, that you
may declare the praises of him who called you out
of darkness into his wonderful light" (1 Peter 2:9).
"His divine power has given us everything we
need for a godly life through our knowledge of

him who called us by his own glory and goodness"
(2 Peter 1:3).

"Now it is God who makes both us and you stand
firm in Christ. He anointed us, set His seal of
ownership on us, and put his Spirit in our hearts as
a deposit, guaranteeing what is to come" (2 Corin-
thians 1:21-22).

This is amazing. He chose you, and He chose me. He called
us to be His. And He did it for a purpose. He chose us, so we
will declare His praises. Tell the whole world Who called us out
of our darkness, out of the darkness of the world, into His light.
He wants a relationship with you. He chose you for it, called you
to it, and sealed you with His Holy Spirit.

You Are Protected

"Be strong and courageous. Do not be afraid; do
not be discouraged, for the Lord your God will be
with you wherever you go" (Joshua 1:9).

"'Though the mountains be shaken, and the hills
be removed, yet my unfailing love for you will
not be shaken, nor my covenant of peace be
removed,'" says the Lord, who has compassion on
you" (Isaiah 54:10).

"Fear not, for I have redeemed you; I have called
you by name, you are mine. When you pass through
the waters, I will be with you; and through the

rivers, they shall not overwhelm you; when you walk through fire, you shall not be burned, and the flame shall not consume you. For I am the Lord your God, the Holy One of Israel, your Savior" (Isaiah 43:1-3).

When your mountains are shaking. When your hills are removed. When you pass through the waters. When you walk through the fire. He is with you. He is protecting you.

Through custody battles, visitation with a parent who has hurt them in the past, trying to get through daily life. Through piles of bills, too many decisions, and lonely nights. He never leaves.

We face so many battles as single moms. I know in my heart and soul that God is with me and protecting my children and me. And yet it doesn't always look that way, does it?

I think of Annie, who went to court to press charges against the man who took her to the brink of death. I think of the intense injustice that he wasn't convicted, never served a day in jail for what he did to her because the other women he had hurt were too afraid to testify. Afraid that they would be next.

The injustice of it all can make us angry and bitter if we let it. But if we look at it through the lens of God's love, of God's character, we can trust that He knows what He is doing. We can trust that He will serve justice one day and that until that day, He will walk with us through each trial.

Annie was never alone in her struggle. God provided for her each step of the way. God walked with her every day. And now He is using her to give a voice and healing to other domestic abuse survivors. Women who need to hear that they, too, are loved and worth loving.

If you are reading this and wondering what in the world I am talking about with God's steadfast, unending love, I want you to know that you can have it, too. It's never too late.

If God is pressing on your heart, asking you to choose Him, maybe today is your day to start over on a new path of following Him. I can promise you it isn't easy. Following God doesn't suddenly make your problems go away or make your path smooth.

It does mean that you will have access to grace and forgiveness and love and strength beyond your wildest imagination.

It means that you will never walk alone, ever again.

Connections
Which one of these truths about God's love means
the most to you? Do these verses change
the way you see yourself?

First Step Forward
Write out some of your favorite verses from this chapter,
and remember God's Word is talking about you.

1.

2.

3.

NOT OVER YET

CHAPTER 31

Choosing Hope

The Merriam Webster dictionary defines hope this way: (noun) desire accompanied by expectation of or belief in fulfillment.

(Intransitive verb) to cherish a desire with anticipation: to want something to happen or be true.

Basically, as the world sees it, a hope is a wish. Nothing more. Nothing to base it on. Just a wish. Thank goodness there is a difference between worldly hope and biblical hope. In a Beth Moore study a few years ago, I heard the definition of biblical hope as "Anxious Expectation." Anxiously expect that there will be enough food. Anxiously expect that God will heal. Anxiously expect God to show up in your circumstances, no matter how dire.

> He is still and will always be in control, no matter what circumstances we face.

I think there is an equally important second part to this kind of hope—trust in God that if He doesn't answer our prayers the way we want Him to, He is still good and still has a plan for our lives. He is still and will always be in control, no matter what circumstances we face.

What's going on in your single mom life right now? What situation has you at a complete loss as to what to do next? What situation do you have absolutely no control over?

I wonder what it looks like from God's perspective. Another chance for Him to make Himself known in your life? Another chance for the world to see that you will praise Him in spite of your circumstances? Another chance for Him to do what only He can do and turn our ashes into beauty?

It's so easy to get stuck looking at unsolvable problems, especially if they haven't been resolved after many prayers and much waiting. But we can change our perspective and remember that God can and will use everything for His glory and our good. We can hold on with biblical hope.

And we will get a front-row seat to see how He will work and be glorified in it.

I'm sure you have seen them. Know them. Maybe you've been one of them. They're the single moms who never recovered, never moved on. The ones who hold on to the pain and regret and fear. The ones who don't see the joy. Who struggle every day. When I see them, I want to give them a great big hug and point them to Christ, who can make all things new. I want them to reach for hope and find a way to start over. And I want to make sure you don't take that path.

I know this road is hard. Sometimes I ache for a husband or for a particular problem to be resolved. I wonder if God has that in His plan for us. But I don't want to get stuck in the wondering, in the wishing, in the regret.

This is our one shot at life. Our one chance to raise our children well and teach them by example how to build a beautiful life in the midst of adversity.

Listen, we all have it. Not one person gets to walk through this life and get to the end unscathed. It doesn't happen. No matter how charmed someone else's life may look, trust me, we don't see it all.

My friend, Holly, jokes about being Job. Wow, has she gone through it. You name it, and Holly or her children have probably experienced it. And it's hard. She will freely admit that each new wave of distress that comes at her is hard. Some of them are so unexpected they send her reeling.

But guess what? Holly lives out the joy of the Lord. I mean, seriously lives it out. She is generous and kind and full of life. No one leaves her house without a hug. No one. Every person that encounters her knows they are seen. Important. Loved.

Do you know why? Holly makes a choice. A choice we all get to make of whether we are going to stay stuck in our struggles or seek out joy and hope wherever we can. I have that choice, and you have that choice. I am working hard to choose joy in my daily life as much as I can. I have found a few things that really help me find hope and joy.

Gathering Gratitude

I bought Post-it Notes® in the happiest colors I could find and am writing notes on them of things I am grateful for. Whether it's a bill being paid off or a kind word from my kids, each note holds special meaning for me, a simple joy to help brighten any day.

I am putting them inside my cupboard doors, tucked away just for me. I am so excited to open those doors and be able to look back at all the blessings.

Walking by the closed cupboard door, knowing the notes are there, reminds me of the blessings hidden inside and makes me smile. I love the difference this is making in my outlook each day and what it is teaching my kiddos.

Always look for the good. It's there; we need to have eyes to see it.

Make Time for God

I know how busy our days are. Endless to do lists, work, school, and parenting make us feel like we have no time left over. What makes all the difference in my days is when I make time for a little talk with God before starting out.

School recently started, and my girls now get on the bus really early in the morning. Early enough that I get to see the sunrise on my walk back from the bus stop. That means I suddenly have a little time in the morning after they leave and before I go to work.

Trust me, there are a million things I feel I should be doing. Laundry, dishes, work, writing. Something productive.

Instead, I started forcing myself to take some time to read my Bible and pray. Some mornings it's very short, a few minutes, really. Some days I get lost in what I am reading and have to rush off once I finish.

Those small moments are making a huge difference for me. Taking the time to give the day to God, ask Him to guard my words, and ask Him for wisdom changes my whole outlook on the day.

Don't Do it Alone

When we are alone too much, our thoughts can run away with us. Our regrets or wishes can take over and send us spiraling. Having someone to reach out to in those moments is critical.

Find other single moms who understand what your life is like and who understand your struggles. Find married couples with kids about the same age as yours and begin building friendships. Reach out to your neighbors.

Just tonight, I had a really tough time with one of my kids. Disrespect, lying, blaming.

I was so hurt and upset by her actions. Then my best friend texted. In my answer to her, I could feel all my frustration changing my outlook. Then she made me laugh. One little comment from her broke that cycle and helped me pull back out and reach for hope.

Find your people. It's so worth it!

Your people will help you see and choose hope when you are too tired to find it on your own. Choosing hope is not easy. So many issues that come with being a single mom try to derail our hope (and our sanity!). We need to make a conscious effort, a purposeful choice, to be hopeful.

Our kids are watching and learning every day. Let's show them how to choose true hope and joy in every circumstance.

Connections

What is one situation that immediately
douses any flicker of hope? What can you do
to counter it next time it happens?

First Step Forward

Plan out three things you can do each day
to help you choose hope.

1.

2.

3.

Cast Your Cares

"Cast all your anxiety on Him because He cares for you" (1 Peter 5:7).

This is such a great action and SO hard to do! Well, not so much the casting part; I seem to be OK with that. It's the "not taking it back to worry about some more" that I have a problem with. God didn't say, "Show me your problems, but you still hang on to them." Or, "Give them to me, but make sure you take them back to check on them every day. He said to "cast all your cares on Him."

Any chance you have a similar struggle? Do you keep worrying and working and stressing about the same challenges over and over? It is such a waste of our time and energy, which are two things that are typically in short supply anyway.

There are so many things we can worry about as single moms. And worrying about them won't change anything. We won't solve them by worrying; we won't delay them by worrying. We'll only wear ourselves out.

Maybe it's time to try a new tactic.

There are two important pieces of this verse. First of all, the word "cast." Dictionary.com defines "cast" like this: a. to throw or hurl; fling; b. to throw off or away.

Did you catch that? Hurl. Fling. We're not talking about tossing something gently aside onto a pile of things to deal with later.

When I think of flinging something, I think of something I want to get rid of in a hurry, and I don't want back. Like that time that I found a spider crawling on me while I was driving, and it took everything in me to not fling it instantly and end up flinging the car, too.

I have some big concerns that I can't seem to fling onto God and not take back. Even when I am not actively worrying about them, they seem to be constantly on my mind as I wrestle to find solutions.

I wanted to set aside my worry, so I wrote a note to God. I wrote out four things that I couldn't solve, and I read the note aloud to Him. My list of things I need help with. Things that are beyond my control and that I spend way too much of my time thinking about. Then I tucked it up on my mantel.

A few times a week, I'd see a corner of the paper and think, Oh, yes, God, please work on those things. I am leaving them with you.

There is peace for me in that. The physical note lying there reminding me that God is working on it, even when I don't see the progress. Even when I get tired of asking.

The Bible says the Holy Spirit intercedes for us with groans we can't understand (Romans 8:26). That note is also my way of giving those problems to the Holy Spirit and asking Him to do His job with them. To continue praying for those struggles, as I go about the rest of my life.

And guess what. I read it again after a couple of months and saw that He had already taken care of two of the four struggles.

Keeping a log, or even a note, of these answered prayers, makes a major difference in my trust. Trust is easier when we can see and remember how He has moved in the past.

After all, that's the second part of the verse. We aren't casting our cares onto someone who is indifferent. We aren't casting our cares onto someone who is powerless to help us. We are casting our cares onto God because He cares for us.

Strong's Concordance explains the second use of "cares" in this verse as a primary verb; to be of interest to, i.e., to concern; take care.

Did you notice it? There are two definitions of the original Greek word. God cares about us, and He takes care of us. His heart is concerned with us, and He has the ability and the desire to live out that care.

We have no need to hold onto our worries.

"Do not be anxious about anything, but in everything by prayer and supplication with thanksgiving, let your requests be made known to God. And the peace of God, which surpasses all understanding, will guard your hearts and your minds in Christ Jesus" (Philippians 4:6-7 ESV)

The God of the universe, Who created us and knows us intimately, loves us, and wants to take care of us. That means we can lay our burdens on Him, the One who has the power to carry them and the wisdom and vision to know what to do about them. Hallelujah!

I have other pressing needs that have come up—things I have taken to God and taken back. I am going to write a new note and physically leave those things with God. A continual reminder that He is working behind the scenes all the time.

I challenge you to give it a try and actually write out your worries, read them to God and leave them somewhere as a constant reminder that He is working. See if you find peace in the reminder as God promised we would.

Connections

What are some situations in your life that you worry about a lot? How would your days change if you let God handle them instead?

First Step Forward

Write a note to God with your worries and put it where you will see it and be reminded that He is working.

1.

2.

3.

CHAPTER 33

God Moments

For many years, I led a Bible study for single moms at my church. Every week, I asked the ladies to share their God Moments: big and small ways they saw God show up in their lives that week.

Sometimes they struggled to see those events. The women got so bogged down in their everyday struggles that they forgot to notice God walking with them through each day. I had been sharing God Moments for so long and training myself to notice God moving in big and small ways in my life that I could almost always find something to say. Where we focus makes all the difference.

When we actively look for God Moments, we can see them all around us:

In the friend who dropped off dinner without knowing what a hard day it had been.

In the message reminding us of something good that we were a part of when the rest of life made us wonder if we had any impact at all.

In the friend willing to sit with us in our hardest moments and celebrate with us in our times of success.

God arranged it all.

Now I see Him almost everywhere. Knowing He is caring for us, knowing He is aware of every need and every desire, knowing that we matter to Him makes it easier to see His action in our lives.

God Moments

I have watched God provide in amazing and everyday ways in our lives and the lives of other single moms. A single mom I know came to me about an area of mold in her basement. She had no idea how to take care of it, was working two jobs and raising three children. I mentioned it in my small group at church. Within a week, a man from our church went to her home and took care of it for her. All we had to do was ask. They had to know there was a need before they could meet it.

> He has us in His hands and won't ever let go.

Last week, God filled our cupboards. I mean, someone literally showed up and gave us so much food that it took me two hours to rearrange the cupboards to squeeze it all in. God will provide. He has promised to provide for all of our needs. And last week?

Well, that felt like God showing off. Reminding me through an over-the-top experience that He has us in His hands and won't ever let go.

The best part was the lesson for my girls. They got to see us receive an overwhelming blessing. A crazy big provision that even included special treats thoughtfully chosen for them. Items

I would never have considered asking anyone for that I usually wouldn't purchase.

Food and snacks and treats we wouldn't have to buy for months afterward. Our joy was bubbling out as laughter as we kept rearranging and finagling to get every last item put away.

Over the years, single moms have told me so many amazing stories of God's provision. I started a collection of their God Moments to remind us all that God will never leave us. Here are a few of my favorites.

Holly's Story: Tina the Minivan

I have a minivan named Tina. Tina has been around the block over 2,000,000 times. Literally. Tina has 224,000 miles on her and quite a story. When I was a single mom struggling to make ends meet, I reached a crossroads. I was working two jobs, raising three kids, and my van broke down. I needed that van to get to work since I lived in an area without public transportation.

So, I asked my Bible study leader if our church would be willing to help me.

They were.

The church met with me and learned about my situation and my van. One of the pastors thought that the best financial decision was to fix the van, so the church paid to have it fixed for me. Six years (and countless miles) later, the van is still running.

Years after they fixed it, after I was remarried, I used it to carry food when I made dinner for ten single moms and their kids at church every Wednesday. Another single mom used it for a couple of months after an accident totaled her car.

Tina was used to transport a team from a ministry in Uganda that were visiting the U.S. God provided, not just for me, but for so many others by the church caring for me and fixing my van.

Samantha's Story: The Mystery Money

When my husband left, we were thousands of dollars in debt. I struggled to keep making minimum payments on our credit cards, never quite sure how I would make it to the end of the month.

A few months later, I received $200 in the mail. The very next day, I found out I owed $238 in taxes. To this day, I don't know who the money came from or how I would have paid that bill without it. God actually provided for me BEFORE I knew there was a need.

Barb's Story – Underground Water

I noticed a large crack in my sidewalk and some water coming up through it. The public works department told me it was a major problem, and since it was on my property, it would be my responsibility to fix it. That meant digging up the sidewalk, doing the repairs underground, and replacing the sidewalk.

That's my great big God who is powerful enough to hold all the stars in His hand and personal enough to want to thrill us with His love.

I had no idea where to start and couldn't even begin to think about how I would pay for such a costly repair. I needed my money to keep food on the table; there was no way I could pay thousands of dollars for this. I was embarrassed and afraid and didn't tell anyone what was going on.

Finally, after several threatening letters from the public works department, I went to work and couldn't hold the tears in anymore. A concerned co-worker asked what was wrong, then said he knew someone who owned a company that fixed these exact issues and asked if I would let him help. Of course, I said yes.

As soon as the owner of that business heard about the situation, he took over. He came to my house, read all the letters, and got to work. He dealt with the legal side of the paperwork and brought his crew out to fix the actual problem.

The repair would have cost me $10,000, and he never asked me to pay a single penny. I was overwhelmed with gratitude. I kept coming to the front door and looking out at the workers, amazed.

Each time I did, they would call out Bible verses to me! I have never seen the church be the hands and feet of Christ more clearly.

My Story: And Then There Was Light

I am renting a duplex right now. It has a bright, beautiful sunroom and we love it here. There is also an issue with the electricity. I am guessing it must spike now and then because sometimes we flip a light switch, and the light bulb pops. Broken. No more light.

This is not a rare occurrence. It happens every couple of weeks.

I finally stopped replacing the light bulbs. If they only last a couple of weeks, it gets pretty expensive to keep changing them. We were down to one or two lightbulbs in our ceiling lights that should have four bulbs. It was darker than we would have liked, but we learned to deal with it.

Until two days ago, one of my girls and I were walking through a local thrift store on our mom and daughter outing.

We found curtains I'd wanted for years for our living room and curtains for her newly rearranged bedroom.

And light bulbs. Brand new LED, energy-efficient light-bulbs for 99¢ a box. Seriously.

I cautiously bought only two boxes, expecting that light bulbs that cheap must not be any good. Plus, they were only 40 watts. But I figured four light bulbs at forty watts each would still be way brighter than our one light bulb.

I filled up one ceiling fan with light bulbs and flipped the switch. Wow! LED lightbulbs that are 40 watts are a lot brighter than old-school light bulbs. I hoped so hard that they would have some left the next day. As soon as I could the next morning, I went back to the thrift store. The parking lot was filled with cars, more than I had ever seen there. I figured with that many customers, the lightbulbs must be gone by now.

I grabbed a cart and headed to the back of the store where the lightbulbs had been. I held my breath as I walked around the corner and then stopped short. There must have been twice as many lightbulbs as the night before.

I stocked up!

I'm sure people were wondering what was up with the crazy lady, grinning from ear to ear as she filled her cart with light-bulbs and nothing else. We now have 14 boxes of regular light bulbs and 11 light bulbs for the recessed lighting. I put four of them in so far, and WOW! is our kitchen bright. It's amazing.

I absolutely know that was God. He knows I need to be frugal. He knows how much I want to make a haven for my girls.

He also knows I want my daughter's bedroom to be beau-tiful and a safe, warm place for her. We had looked at Target for curtains and couldn't possibly spend enough to buy brand new ones. Instead, He provided gorgeous curtains in her favorite color that match the dresser someone gave us.

That's not an accident.

That's not the universe conspiring or the planets aligning.

That's my great big God who is powerful enough to hold all the stars in His hand and personal enough to want to thrill us with His love. The God who is in charge of everything yet bends down to step into our world and care for us.

Life is so much sweeter when we see God's hand of protection and provision. When we see Him care for our needs and even our wants. We have lived fine without much light and without pretty curtains. And it's lovely that He provided for both of those desires.

I have seen Him provide in so many ways over the years.

That's what these God Moments are: times when other single moms and I have watched God provide or protect or thrill us with His love. These are memories to start collecting for when it's harder to see His provision and feel His presence.

The hope I have is rooted in who God is, in how I have seen Him move in my life before, in being able to trust His Word because I choose to and because I have found Him to be completely trustworthy and true.

So now it's your turn.

Maybe you want to take some bright and colorful Post-it Notes® and write notes to yourself when God does something cool.

Stick them inside your cupboards, so you see them each day. Or line them along your mirror. Or keep a family journal of God's faithfulness.

One tradition I am starting with my girls is to have a jar of God Moments. We have fun colored card stock, and we each get to write down when God does something good in our lives, then put the paper in the jar. On New Year's Eve each year, we are going to read the notes to remind ourselves of God's faithfulness to us throughout the year.

It takes practice. There are times of struggle when our emotions make it harder to see the good. To see God moving. From experience, I know He always is. I challenge you to start your own tradition of hope, so you and your children can look back on God's faithfulness to your family. There is nothing more certain to provide hope than the remembrance of how God has shown up in your life in the past.

"Every good and perfect gift is from above" (James 1:17).

Even matching curtains and cheap lightbulbs.

Connections

How has God moved in your life in the past?
Can you see Him working even today?

First Step Forward

Start by writing a recent God Moment from your own life here. Then get a notebook or Post-it Notes® to begin your own God Moment collection.

Epilogue

"But you, Lord, are a shield around me, my glory, the One who lifts my head high. I call out to the Lord, and he answers me from his holy mountain" (Psalm 3:3-4).

Precious One, there is so much that lies before you. So much life and love and hope and joy. When you are discouraged, I want you to feel God lifting your chin so you can look Him full in the face.

I want you to know that He sees you. Truly sees you.

Sees every single care that is weighing you down.

Sees your hopes and dreams for the future.

Sees your scars and wounds and knows every battle you have been through.

He stood next to you in each one, and He will never turn away. Let Him look deep in your eyes. Feel His love pouring out over you. You are so precious to Him. So very loved. Nothing will ever change that. Stand in that today. Stand in your belovedness.

Let it make you stand a little taller. Hold your head a little higher. Know all the way to your toes that He loves you madly. He rejoices over you. He made you to bring Him joy. You bring Him joy! What an amazing truth. He wants your joy to be complete. Deep-down, soul-level joy. He wants to know you. He wants a relationship with you.

Let Him lift your chin and speak His truth over you. You will never be the same.

I'll be right here cheering you on.

Resources

Check out these resources to help you escape an abusive situation and start over.

National Domestic Violence Hotline:
www.thehotline.org
1-800-799-7233

Domestic Shelters: www.domesticshelters.org
Domestic Shelters offers many resources, including:
    Find a local women's shelter
    How to file a protection order
    Checklist of what essentials to pack when leaving an
        abusive situation
    Helping children cope after abuse
    How to move forward after abuse
    Legal help for Domestic Violence Issues

Battered Women's Justice Project:
bwjp.org, 800-903-0111, prompt 1 to speak to an advocate

WomensLaw: www.womenslaw.org
Offers plain language legal information for victims of abuse.
Resources that are searchable by state:
    Advocates and Shelters
    Finding a lawyer
    Courthouse locations
    Sheriff Departments (for protection orders)

Peace with God

God loves you. He wants to be in relationship with you. Because of sin, that relationship is broken and the only way to heal it is through the redemption made possible by Jesus Christ when he died in our place on the cross.

If you want to know more or want to begin your relationship with Jesus, the Billy Graham Evangelical Association is a great place to start. https://peacewithgod.net

Notes

Chapter 12
1. "Post-traumatic stress disorder (PTSD)", Accessed December 4, 2021 https://www.mayoclinic.org/diseases-conditions/post-traumatic-stress-disorder/symptoms-causes/syc-20355967

2. "Depression (major depressive disorder)", Accessed December 4, 2021 https://www.mayoclinic.org/diseases-conditions/depression/symptoms-causes/syc-20356007

3. "Generalized anxiety disorder" Accessed December 4, 2021, https://www.mayoclinic.org/diseases-conditions/generalized-anxiety-disorder/symptoms-causes/syc-20360803

Chapter 16
4. Caitlin Crawshaw. 2018. "Co-parenting after you've left an abusive relationship." todaysparent. Accessed December 4, 2021. https://www.todaysparent.com/family/parenting/co-parenting-after-youve-left-an-abusive-relationship/

Chapter 18
5. Karyn B. Purvis, Ph.D., David R. Cross, Ph.D., and Wendy Lyons Sunshine, The Connected Child (McGraw-Hill, 2007), 48

Chapter 20
6. Karyn Purvis Institute of Child Development. "Dr. Karyn Purvis." Texas Christian University. Accessed December 3, 2021. https://child.tcu.edu/karyn/#sthash.JUHTwMdT.dpbs.

7. Karyn B. Purvis, Ph.D., David R. Cross, Ph.D., and Wendy Lyons Sunshine, The Connected Child (McGraw-Hill, 2007), 50

Chapter 24
8. National Education Association/CDC. 2021 "Trauma Informed Schools." Accessed December 3, 2021. https://www.nea.org/professional-excellence/student-engagement/trauma-informed-schools (image description of trauma brain)

9. Dr. Caroline Leaf. (No date available). "Why mind-management is the solution to cleaning up your mental mess." https://cdn.shopify.com/s/files/1/1810/9163/files/General_White_Paper_100720_final_version.pdf?v=1602124109.

10. Dr. Caroline Leaf. (No date available). "Why mind-management is the solution to cleaning up your mental mess." https://cdn.shopify.com/s/files/1/1810/9163/files/General_White_Paper_100720_final_version.pdf?v=1602124109.

11. Dr. Caroline Leaf, "Deconstructing trauma & how to find healing through learning + how we should talk to kids about mental health (with Lewis Howes)" Cleaning up the Mental Mess (podcast), August 19, 2021, 16:22.

12. Rick Hanson "How to Grow the Good in Your Brain", Greater Good, September 24, 2013 https://greatergood.berkeley.edu/article/item/how_to_grow_the_good_in_your_brain

13. Jon Acuff, Soundtracks (Baker Books, 2021), 35

Gratitude

To the single moms who shared their stories with me, wanting to help other single moms.

To Everyone who came alongside us on our crisis day: Wendy, Mom, Uncle Dick, Claire, Kevin, Tara. I am so grateful for your presence in person and on the phone to steady me when I felt as if my world had fallen apart.

To Pam, whose home became our haven. Thank you for listening for so many hours and for your constant strength and presence during those difficult days. Thanks to Kaelyn, Rachel, and Daniel for making Frankie feel like the most important kid in the world when we visited. Thank you, Rick, for always being willing to help.

To Ruth for your steady presence in our lives.

To my Tuesday morning Bible Study ladies. You are all so precious to me. I am so grateful Katie didn't want to go to study alone years ago. I had no idea what blessings God had in store through you all.

To Deb for your ever-present wisdom and love for me and my girls. And for making me laugh when laughter seems far away. You lighten my load immeasurably.

To my kids for bringing me joy, laughter and love. I will love you forever and always, no matter what. Watch out for deer. +1

About the Author

Stephanie is a relentless cheerleader for single moms from all walks of life. She has been a single mom for over a decade and has experienced the challenges and beauty of this crazy, amazing life. Stephanie wants to give those behind her on this journey a head start, with encouragement that was missing during the early years of her own journey. She has been writing for much of her life and has been putting her words out into the world for 15 years. Stephanie had one biological child when she became a single mom and has since adopted a child from Uganda. The three of them live in Wisconsin with their dogs, Bella and Keva, and three fish.

Let's Connect!

Find Stephanie online at:

www.stephaniebartelt.com

authorstephaniebartelt

loveunrationed

Please leave a Review!

Stephanie wants the message of *Not Over Yet* to reach as many single moms as possible. You can help by telling others about the book and by leaving a review at amazon.com, bn.com, goodreads.com, and wherever you find books online.